THE COMPLETE VEGAN INSTANT POT® COOKBOOK

THE COMPLETE
VEGAN
INSTANT POT®
COOKBOOK

101 DELICIOUS WHOLE-FOOD RECIPES FOR YOUR PRESSURE COOKER

BARB MUSICK

PHOTOGRAPHY BY EVI ABELER

ROCKRIDGE
PRESS

INSTANT POT® and associated logos are owned by Instant Brands Inc. and are used under license.

For general information on our other products and services or to obtain technical support, please contact our Customer Care Department within the U.S. at (866) 744-2665, or outside the U.S. at (510) 253-0500.

Rockridge Press publishes its books in a variety of electronic and print formats. Some content that appears in print may not be available in electronic books, and vice versa.

Interior and Cover Designer: Joshua Moore
Photo Art Director: Sue Smith
Editor: Bridget Fitzgerald
Production Editor: Andrew Yackira
Photography: Photography © 2019 Evi Abeler. Food styling by Albane Sharrard. Author photo courtesy of Angela Prodanova.

ISBN: Print 978-1-64152-162-8
eBook 978-1-64152-163-5

FOR THE ANIMALS:

You're the reason I went vegan and the reason
I'll never stop trying to change the world.

Red Thai Curry
Cauliflower, page 108

CONTENTS

———

INTRODUCTION

IT'S AN AMAZING TIME to be vegan! We have access to all manner of fresh fruits and vegetables, grains and legumes—from sources both local and global. We have meat and dairy substitutes that early vegans could only dream of and the ability to order anything we want and have it delivered to our doorstep. Then we get to combine these wonderful ingredients into meals, and that's where the Instant Pot® comes in. Once thought of as an intimidating appliance, or only for meat dishes, the pressure cooker has come a long way and is now a beloved fixture in many home kitchens, especially those focused on plant-based cooking. The multifunction features of the Instant Pot®, in particular, have given the modern vegan cook the ability to make healthy and delicious meals as efficiently as possible.

I'll admit it: I was not an early adopter of pressure cooking. I thought, "Why add another appliance to my collection?" But, I'm so thankful I decided to purchase that Instant Pot® because it has changed the way I cook. Longtime vegans who want to eat more unprocessed foods (Me! You, too?), newly minted vegans looking for inspiration, and people who just want to add more plant-based recipes to their diet can all benefit from adding this method of easy, healthy, and hearty cooking to their regular routines.

When people first consider the Instant Pot®, they usually focus on how quickly it cooks. And yes, it often does cook meals faster than other methods, but that's not my favorite thing about it. The way I see it, its biggest value is how it saves you from being tied to the kitchen for long periods of time. There's no need to hover over the stove or continuously stir the risotto. It frees you up to leave the kitchen and do other things while the pot takes care of the cooking. The Instant Pot® gives you some of your time back, time you can dedicate to other things that are important to you—whether that's cuddling with a loved one, binge-watching Netflix, working on an art project, or organizing your sock drawer (no judgment here!).

The recipes in this book focus on fresh, whole foods. They don't require a lot of unusual ingredients, and they aren't overly complicated. As someone who didn't really learn to cook until my thirties, I absolutely mean it when I say, "If I can make these, so can you!" These healthy dishes are based on fruits, vegetables, grains, nuts, and legumes—and I'm so excited to share them with you!

1

THE COMPLETE
APPLIANCE

THE BENEFITS OF vegan pressure cooking are almost too numerous to count. The Instant Pot® allows us to prepare our favorite meals much more quickly, and this reduced cooking time means grains, beans, and vegetables are able to retain more of their flavor and nutrients—so meals made with these ingredients are tastier and healthier. Home cooks who use the Instant Pot® will also see cost savings. In addition to the money you can save with simple steps, such as quickly cooking dried beans instead of buying canned, pressure cooking also uses less energy than stovetop and oven cooking. But above all, the Instant Pot® drastically reduces the amount of time you are tethered to the kitchen. While your meal is cooking away, you're free to do whatever you'd rather be doing—or at least check a few items off your to-do list. I'm convinced these benefits will make the Instant Pot® the most essential item in your vegan kitchen.

Vegan Instant Pot® 101

Yes, there are a lot of buttons on the front of your Instant Pot®, but don't let that overwhelm you. It is really quite easy to use, as you'll soon see. These settings have all been designed to make the busy home cook's life a little less hectic, whether you're using your Instant Pot® for quick weeknight meals, parties, or meal prep.

There are several models of the Instant Pot®, some with more advanced functionality and options, so I encourage you to spend some quality time with the user manual for your particular version. But to get you started, here is an overview of some of the most commonly used settings.

MANUAL (OR PRESSURE COOK), PRESSURE, AND ADJUST

I have friends who never use any other setting than this one: the simple, timed pressure cook. This setting allows you to bypass the specialty settings and choose the correct pressure level and cook time for your recipe. The settings available to you in Manual mode are:

HIGH PRESSURE: Many plant-based foods are best cooked at high pressure, including beans and grains. This is one of the most common settings you'll find in Instant Pot® recipes.

LOW PRESSURE: I utilize this option for vegetables that can cook quickly at a lower temperature, such as cauliflower and asparagus. The lower temperature, combined with a shorter cook time (sometimes 0 minutes!) keeps the veggies from becoming mushy.

SLOW COOKER/SIMMER: Why keep an extra appliance in your kitchen when the Instant Pot® is a slow cooker, too? Use this function for any slow cooker recipe, or to simmer dishes you want to keep warm, such as soups or chilis.

SAUTÉ/BROWN: I use this setting for many of my recipes. I love the ability to sauté vegetables (especially garlic and onion) right in the pressure cooker—it saves the extra step (and dirty pan) of doing it on the stovetop.

SPECIALTY SETTINGS

The following specialty functions are also available on all Instant Pot® models, although the names may vary. The interesting thing about these settings is that although they're more specialized than Manual, they offer the cook slightly less control over the dish. Depending on the Instant Pot® you have, you may be able to toggle between Low and High Pressure on some, but not all, specialty settings.

BEAN/CHILI: An easy way to cook beans, but double-check the recipe, as not all beans require the same amount of time to cook.

MULTIGRAIN: This setting is generally known as the go-to for brown and wild rice. It includes a high-temperature soaking phase that is helpful with these tougher grains.

COMMON MISTAKES

Use this advice to avoid the frustration of committing some of the most common Instant Pot® goofs:

1 FORGETTING TO TURN THE STEAM RELEASE HANDLE TO "SEALING" I've definitely done this! To avoid, make this inspection part of your process: Double-check that the handle is in the correct position every time you put the lid on.

2 NOT CLEANING THE SEALING RING The silicone ring is what allows the pressure to build and cook your food so quickly, but it can also collect odors. Luckily it is easy to remove and is dishwasher safe!

3 OVERFILLING THE INNER POT When pressure cooking, never fill the pot more than two-thirds full, or half full if your ingredients will release a lot of liquid while cooking. An Instant Pot® with too much liquid is at risk for releasing hot liquid through the pressure release valve, which can result in burns.

4 FORGETTING TO REPLACE THE INNER POT BEFORE ADDING INGREDIENTS Oops! If you've done this, hopefully it was something dry and easy to clean up. Be sure to thoroughly clean all ingredients out of the Instant Pot® before replacing the inner pot and starting over.

5 USING A QUICK RELEASE FOR GRAINS OR BEANS Quick releasing the pressure immediately after grains or beans have finished cooking is an easy way to burn yourself, as spatter is likely. Start with a natural release and, if you must use quick release, wear silicone gloves or use a wooden spoon to move the handle so as to avoid injury.

INSTANT POT® FAQS

I had a ton of questions when I first entered the world of pressure cooking, and I'm sure you do, too. Here are some Instant Pot® FAQs I hope you'll find useful, whether you're a new user or an old pro.

Are recipe cooking times exact? *The correct cooking time for any recipe can vary based on a number of factors from big picture (your altitude—I live in Colorado, so this is a big factor) to small (how ripe your ingredients are), so it's best to look at cooking times as a range. The good news is, pressure cooking tends to be forgiving, and if your dish needs a few more minutes to finish, functions like Sauté or Slow Cooker give you options.*

So many recipes call for the Manual button, but my Instant Pot® doesn't have one. What should I do? *Some newer models of the Instant Pot® have replaced Manual with Pressure Cook . . . but they do exactly the same thing!*

Why does my Instant Pot® steam and hiss while it comes to pressure? *Double-check that the pressure release handle is set to Sealing—and then relax. It's normal for some steam and/or a hissing sound to escape from the valve as the Instant Pot® comes to pressure.*

Why is my Instant Pot® making a popping noise while cooking? *This happens when there is moisture on the outside of the inner pot. Always make sure the pot is completely dry on the outside and bottom before putting it into the Instant Pot®. Don't worry, though, the noise will stop when the moisture is gone.*

Can I double a recipe? *Yes, but it's not an exact science. First and foremost, if the recipe is for beans or grains, you need to be sure that doubling the recipe won't take you over the two-thirds full marker (or half full if your ingredients will release a lot of liquid). Also keep in mind that not all ingredients need to be doubled. Many recipes call for water to be added to the bottom of the pot (if you're cooking with a steam basket or baking dish atop the trivet, for instance). That amount of water almost never needs to be doubled.*

Can I convert my favorite recipe to the Instant Pot®? *Not every recipe is ideal for pressure cooking, so it's important to take a few factors into consideration. Because the Instant Pot® requires liquid to come to pressure, recipes that already contain liquid (soups, chilis, grains) are simple to convert. Conversely, dishes intended to be crispy or fried may not be easily converted.*

Can I use my Instant Pot® for pressure canning? *There are a lot of opinions online regarding this, but the brand's official website states they do not recommend using their product for pressure canning.*

What do I do if there's too much liquid? *When you've released the pressure and removed the lid, you may find more liquid than you anticipated. Simply select the Sauté Low function and cook until you've reached the desired consistency. Just be sure to stir so nothing burns.*

PORRIDGE: I use this setting for making some of my breakfast recipes, but I use the Manual function just as often.

RICE: As with the bean setting, I find this setting to be a little too generic. There are so many different types of rice that have different cook times, so I tend to stick with Manual.

SOUP: Worried about your soup burning? This setting compensates for the fact that you won't be stirring that soup by keeping the bottom of the inner pot from getting too hot.

STEAM: Use the trivet that comes with your Instant Pot®, or a steamer basket, along with at least 1 cup of water in the bottom to get easy steamed vegetables without the pressure function.

YOGURT: Yes, it even has a yogurt setting! Follow any directions carefully, as these recipes tend to be a bit more complicated.

VEGAN HACKS

The Instant Pot® is an amazing kitchen appliance for everyone, but it can be especially useful for those of us on a vegan diet. Here are my favorite vegan shortcuts for the pressure cooker:

NEVER BUY VEGETABLE STOCK AGAIN. Making your own stock used to take all day—and you had to be nearby to keep an eye on it! With the Instant Pot® you can easily make stock in advance, or as the first step of creating your meal. Check out my recipe for DIY Vegetable Stock (page 154) to get started.

SAVE MONEY. Canned beans may not seem expensive, but they're about twice the cost per serving of dried beans. Purchasing dried beans to cook in your Instant Pot® is an easy way to save on your grocery bill (and they take up less room in your pantry).

KEEP YOUR KITCHEN COOL. The Instant Pot® leaves little reason to turn your oven on. Nearly every vegan recipe you make in the oven can be converted for cooking with pressure, which is great on warm days when you don't want to heat up the house.

"ROUND OUT" LEFTOVERS. Place leftovers into a freezer bag and then into a round container to freeze them into the perfect shape for the Instant Pot®. When you're ready to enjoy that meal again, slide it out of the bag and into your Instant Pot®!

TAKE IT WITH YOU. Visiting family or going on a road trip? The Instant Pot® is a great way to keep food costs down while traveling and to make sure vegan items are available for you. All you need are ingredients and a place to plug it in.

Accessories

A person could go a little crazy with all the accessories available for your Instant Pot®. Some are available for sale through the official Instant Pot® website, but many more are offered by other sellers online and in stores. (It's important to note that some items, such as extra sealing rings, must be purchased from authorized dealers so your warranty isn't voided.) Which accessories are right for you, of course, depends largely on the types of recipes you make on a regular basis, but here are my suggestions for the average Instant Pot® enthusiast.

STAINLESS STEEL STEAMER BASKET WITH SILICONE HANDLE: This was the first accessory I purchased and I use it all the time for steaming vegetables. For under $20 you can get a basket that is compatible with whichever size Instant Pot® you own and that can also be used in a pan on your stovetop.

NONSTICK 2-IN-1 SPRINGFORM/BUNDT PAN: This handy little guy isn't just for baked goods; it's also ideal for lasagna, layered enchiladas, and any other meals you don't want to be "scooping" out of your Instant Pot®. These come in multiple sizes to fit every Instant Pot®.

SILICONE EGG BITE MOLDS: This may seem like a strange suggestion from a vegan, but stay with me! In addition to Kale & Sweet Potato Mini Quiche (page 22), these can be used for any meal you want to prepare in bite-size portions.

OVEN-SAFE GLASS BOWL: Not just for the Instant Pot®, but very useful! I use a 7-cup Pyrex glass bowl regularly.

TEMPERED GLASS LID: You can use a lid from another pot if you have one that fits, but if you use your Instant Pot® frequently for techniques that don't involve pressure, such as steaming, slow cooking, or keeping meals warm, this lid is a great investment. It allows you to see inside and removes easily when you need to stir or taste.

SILICONE GLOVES/MITTS: These keep your fingers safe while quick releasing pressure, and they come in a variety of styles and price points.

Caring for Your Instant Pot®

The Instant Pot® is easy to care for and will last longer if you follow a few simple steps.

- Remove and wash the sealing ring frequently! It is dishwasher safe and washing it is also a good opportunity to check for cracks or other damage, indicating it needs to be replaced immediately.

- You can run the lid through the dishwasher, too, but only on the top rack.

- It's easy to overlook because it's on the back of your Instant Pot®, but don't forget the condensation collector. It doesn't need to be handwashed after each use, but it can get grimy if you ignore it too long.

- Never put your cooker base in the dishwasher or allow it to get wet; just wipe it down with a lightly damp cloth to keep it looking its best.

- To keep everything deodorized, simply fill the inner pot with 1 cup of water, 1 cup of vinegar, and some lemon peels. Select the Steam setting, let it run for 2 to 3 minutes, and let the pressure release naturally. This is a great way to deal with any lingering funky smells.

2

THE VEGAN KITCHEN

UNDER PRESSURE

————

WE'RE ALL EAGER to get to the recipes (this is a cookbook, after all!), but first let's take a closer look at the best foods for pressure cooking, some essential ingredients I think all vegan cooks should keep on hand, and some recipe guidelines to keep in mind.

The Best Foods for Vegan Pressure Cooking

Some foods just seem destined for the pressure cooker, but in reality, *nearly everything* can be cooked quickly and deliciously in this miraculous appliance! Here are a few of my favorites.

VEGETABLES

Vegetables are fantastic for pressure cooking because it allows their natural flavors to develop quickly. Here are a few vegetables I love to pressure cook.

Artichokes

Fibrous veggies, such as the artichoke, pressure cook like a dream. Make them my way (see Steamed Artichokes, page 44), and you'll never cook them on the stovetop again!

Squash

Any kind of squash can go into your Instant Pot®, which is great news when you're craving butternut in the middle of summer and don't want to heat up the kitchen.

Sweet Potatoes

Sure, you can bake a sweet potato and add toppings, but pressure cooking them with extra seasonings multiplies the flavor.

LEGUMES AND GRAINS

Grains and legumes are great in lots of dishes, especially one-pot meals. You can even cook them along with other ingredients. What's easier than that?

Lentils

Speaking of one-pot meals, lentils are excellent in everything and cook quickly in the pressure cooker.

Millet

Millet can be tricky on the stovetop, but it's easy in the pressure cooker—and ready for a variety of sweet and savory recipes.

Rice

This is another example of a simple food that can easily be amped up by cooking with your favorite flavors and spices.

BEANS

I've never met a bean I don't like . . . or that I won't pressure cook. Canned beans are convenient when time is of the essence, but dried beans are more economical and environmentally friendly.

Black

Possibly the most versatile bean out there, the black bean works in nearly every type of cuisine.

Lima

At a mere 1 to 3 minutes cook time for soaked beans, this is the very fastest cooking bean and makes a great addition to soups and casseroles.

Pinto

This is my personal favorite—I just love its versatility. Cook them with spices to heighten their flavor and use them in myriad recipes.

Research has shown that a little cooking can actually increase the nutrient content of some mushrooms—and pressure cooking may be the best method because of the shorter cooking time required!

Baby Bella

Tasty and toothsome, bellas are wonderful in pasta, or on their own as a side dish.

King Oyster

This mushroom's meaty texture has made it a popular seafood substitute in vegan recipes.

White Button

Perfect for making vegan Cream of Mushroom Soup (page 57)!

Essential Ingredients

We all have our trusty go-tos—reliable ingredients and flavors we use over and over because we love them and know they work. Here are a few I recommend keeping on hand in your refrigerator and pantry.

REFRIGERATOR

There's nothing better than a fridge bursting with fresh veggies and vegan proteins. Here are my staples:

Carrots and celery

Combine these with an onion from your pantry and make an easy mirepoix—the flavorful start to many delicious soups.

DIY Vegetable Stock (page 154)

Add this to your meal prep list and keep it on hand for lots of uses. Even better, freeze it in an ice cube tray so you can easily add it to recipes as needed.

Frozen vegetables

Frozen veggies add nutrition to any recipe and they're super affordable.

Kale

Clean and tear your kale in advance—it's so simple to stir into soups and stews after you've released the pressure and opened your Instant Pot®. It wilts in about 1 minute!

Nondairy milk

There is a wide variety of nondairy milks on the market today, some with stronger flavors than others. My hands-down favorite is cashew milk, which is thick and creamy and has a nice mild flavor.

Tempeh

This is an easy way to add that "meaty" texture to chili or hash. Sauté first with a little smoked paprika and it'll taste a bit like bacon.

Tofu, firm

The most versatile ingredient, in my opinion; because it takes on the flavors you cook it in, tofu can work in almost any dish.

Tofu, soft or silken

Blend with a little nondairy milk, salt, and nutritional yeast to create a creamy sauce.

These shelf-stable staples are always useful to have at the ready.

Canned beans

Sometimes canned beans just work better, especially in recipes where they're combined with vegetables with short cooking times.

Dried beans and lentils

They're economical and easy to make in your Instant Pot®, so there's no reason not to keep them on hand.

Good quality oils

I prefer olive and avocado oils, along with a more general vegetable oil (when you don't want a strong flavor).

Kala namak

Sometimes called "black salt," this is the secret ingredient needed to make anything taste like eggs. I utilize it mostly in tofu-based breakfast dishes, although it has many more uses. It is often available in Asian markets and is easy to order online.

Nonstick spray

You'll use this when cooking in baking dishes or pans inside the Instant Pot® and to coat the aluminum foil that covers the food. You should also coat the inside of glass baking dishes. I use an avocado oil–based spray, but any kind will work.

Nutritional yeast

More commonly known as "nooch," this can be added to sauces and scrambles for a cheesy flavor, or just sprinkle atop your favorite pasta in lieu of Parmesan.

Onions

Onion powder is fine, but I love fresh onions in my dishes, especially when they're still a little crunchy.

Raw cashews

Like the soft tofu listed previously, cashews can be used to make everything from Alfredo sauce to sour cream (see page 160)—all vegan!

Sea salt

I'm a lover of all things salt, and while my recipes don't specify a specific type of salt, I always prefer sea salt. It's less heavily processed than table salt (which also contains additives to prevent clumping).

Seasoned salt

There are so many to choose from, so I recommend you find the one that appeals most to your palate. You can also choose one with a flavor profile that works best with the type of dishes you cook most often, such as Italian seasoned salt.

Smoked paprika

This is a magical spice that gives everything a beautiful smoky flavor. I prefer it over liquid smoke.

THE COMPLETE VEGAN BOWL

I have a theory on why bowl-based meals are so popular with plant-based eaters, and it isn't because eating from a bowl is innately more fun than eating from a plate (although it is!). It's actually because it's such an easy way to combine all our favorite ingredients, flavors, and textures into one complete meal. Here are a few combinations you can make in *your* bowl.

COMBO 1

Cilantro Lime Brown Rice *(page 93)* + Black Beans + Mashed Avocado

COMBO 2

Coconut Jasmine Rice *(page 96)* + Asian Veggie Mix + Peanut Sauce

COMBO 3

Brown Rice + Green Chile Chickpeas *(page 89)* + Cashew Sour Cream *(page 160)*

COMBO 4

White Rice + Steamed Veggies + Korean Barbecue Chickpea Tacos *(page 134)*

COMBO 5

Brown Rice + Always Perfect Beets *(page 48)* + Steamed Cauliflower + Tahini Sauce

Kitchen Safety Guide

For best results with your Instant Pot®, follow these guidelines.

- Always wear silicone gloves or mitts when turning the handle for a quick pressure release. If you don't have mitts, a wooden spoon works really well to move the handle while keeping your arm a safe distance from the steam.

- Use caution when opening the lid after the pressure has released. There's still steam in there, so you don't want your face too close when you open it.

- Everything that comes out of the Instant Pot® is really, really hot at first! It may sound silly, but wait a minute or two before tasting. Trust me—I speak from experience.

- Never, ever, ever attempt to force the lid open. Always wait for the pin to drop and the lid to unlock on its own before you carefully open it.

- Don't deep-fry in your Instant Pot®. Heating frying oil under pressure is unsafe and isn't what the Instant Pot® was designed to do.

- Always include at least 1 cup of water in your ingredients. This might be at the bottom of the pot (if you're using the trivet, a steam basket, or other accessory), or mixed in with your other ingredients.

- One of the best things about the Instant Pot® is you aren't required to constantly check on your meal while it is cooking, but that doesn't mean you can leave the house entirely. Stay nearby and do keep an eye on it.

- Replace the sealing ring as soon as it shows signs of damage, or every 18 to 24 months, whichever comes first.

About the Recipes

We're almost to the recipes, and I'm so excited for you to try them! All recipes in this book focus on a "whole foods" approach to eating, by which I mean I use mainly vegetables, fruits, grains, and legumes with few processed ingredients. These are healthy meals you can feed yourself, your family, and your friends and feel really good about it. Before you start adding ingredients to your Instant Pot®, there are just a few things to keep in mind.

It's important to note that these recipes were developed in Denver, Colorado, at an altitude of around 5,000 feet above sea level. If you live at a much lower altitude than I do, your cook times will be a little bit shorter. Or, if you live at a higher altitude, your cook times will be a bit longer. See the handy adjustment chart (page 163) for more details. Throughout the book, I've included both my timing as well as an adjusted time, in parentheses, for those of you closer to sea level (this reflects a 15 percent decrease in pressure cooking time, and slightly shorter oven cooking time). Make sure to adjust as needed for your particular location (again, see the chart on page 163). Here are a few other general cooking guidelines to keep in mind.

- When a recipe instructs you to cook at High or Low Pressure, that means utilizing the Manual (or Pressure Cook, if you have a newer Instant Pot® model) function.

- Don't underestimate cooking times: Although most recipes include prep and cook time, you have to factor in the time it takes for the Instant Pot® to come to pressure. This can add 5 to 15-plus minutes overall, depending on the amount of liquid and ingredients.

- Unless I specify something different, the water added to the bottom of the Instant Pot® in recipes using the trivet or steam basket should always be cold. Using warm or hot water changes the cooking time.

- If the recipe says, "Turn off the Instant Pot®," it literally means that. Hit the Cancel button to keep the cooker from going into Keep Warm mode, which can easily overcook your food!

- Finally, these recipes were all created using a 6-quart Instant Pot®. Cooking times should be the same if you're using a larger version, but it will take longer to come to pressure.

Now it's time to cook! I had so much fun creating these recipes. I hope you enjoy them as much as I do. Thank you for making them part of your vegan kitchen. Cheers!

Fruity Quinoa &
Granola Bowls

3

INSTANT
BREAKFASTS

PREP TIME:
5 minutes

COOKING
SETTING:
Manual, High
Pressure for
8 minutes
(7 minutes at
sea level)

RELEASE:
Natural for
10 minutes,
then Quick

TOTAL TIME:
23 minutes

CINNAMON APPLE PORRIDGE

BUDGET FRIENDLY • GLUTEN FREE • NUT FREE • SOY FREE

This dish requires your decision-making skills: Do you want your apples soft or a little crunchy? You can cook the apples along with the rest of the ingredients if you want them soft, but if you like a crisper consistency, add them at the end. Either way (but especially if you're cooking the apples with the quinoa), topping your bowl with additional fruit, berries, or nuts is a decision you won't regret. **SERVES 4**

1 cup quinoa, rinsed

1½ cups water

2 tablespoons maple syrup

2 tablespoons ground cinnamon

½ teaspoon vanilla extract

¼ to ½ teaspoon salt

1 apple, chopped

½ to 1 cup nondairy milk

1. In your Instant Pot®, stir together the quinoa, water, maple syrup, cinnamon, vanilla, salt, and apple (if you want it soft). Lock the lid and turn the steam release handle to Sealing. Using the Manual function, set the cooker to High Pressure for 8 minutes (7 minutes at sea level).

2. When the cook time is complete, let the pressure release naturally for 10 minutes; quick release any remaining pressure.

3. Carefully remove the lid and stir in as much milk as needed to make it creamy.

4. If you didn't cook the apples, add them now and put the cover back on for 1 to 2 minutes to warm them.

PER SERVING: Calories: 232; Total fat: 4g; Saturated fat: 0g; Sodium: 196mg; Carbs: 45g; Fiber: 6g; Protein: 7g

PEANUT BUTTER & CHOCOLATE STEEL CUT OATS

BUDGET FRIENDLY • GLUTEN FREE • SOY FREE

I'm one of those people who loves eating breakfast for dinner, but this time I decided to switch it up a bit—dessert for breakfast! I always imagined these oats would be perfect for someone who has trouble getting up in the morning. They'd be lured out of bed and into the kitchen, and have already scarfed down the entire bowl before realizing it was oatmeal! **SERVES 4 TO 6**

PREP TIME:
3 minutes

COOKING SETTING:
Manual, High Pressure for 12 minutes (10 minutes at sea level)

RELEASE:
Natural for 10 minutes, then Quick

TOTAL TIME:
25 minutes

2 cups steel cut oats

2½ cups water

2½ cups nondairy milk, divided, plus more as needed

¼ teaspoon salt

¼ cup chocolate chips

¼ cup peanut butter

2 tablespoons agave, or maple syrup

1. In the Instant Pot®, combine the oats, water, 2 cups of milk, the salt, and chocolate chips. Stir to mix. Lock the lid and turn the steam release handle to Sealing. Using the Manual function, set the cooker to High Pressure for 12 minutes (10 minutes at sea level).

2. When the cook time is complete, turn off the pressure cooker. Let the pressure release naturally for 10 minutes; quick release any remaining pressure.

3. Add the remaining ½ cup of milk (more if you want the oats thinner). Stir in the peanut butter and agave (I like my peanut butter in thick swirls!) and enjoy.

TECHNIQUE TIP: Make sure the inner pot of your pressure cooker is never filled more than halfway when cooking oats or the foam may clog the pressure release valve.

PER SERVING: Calories: 357; Total fat: 16g; Saturated fat: 5g; Sodium: 346mg; Carbs: 45g; Fiber: 6g; Protein: 11g

PREP TIME:
2 minutes

COOKING
SETTING:
Manual, High
Pressure for
8 minutes
(7 minutes at
sea level)

RELEASE:
Natural for
10 minutes,
then Quick

TOTAL TIME:
20 minutes

FRUITY QUINOA & GRANOLA BOWLS

I love the variety of textures in this dish, with the warm quinoa and the crunchy granola. It's also really easy to change it up to suit your particular cravings. Add more nondairy milk if you want the quinoa base to be a little creamier, or more maple syrup to satisfy your sweet tooth. Fresh sliced fruit or toasted walnuts on top are a favorite addition of mine. If your local grocer carries vegan yogurt, consider adding some of that, too. **SERVES 4**

1 cup quinoa, rinsed

1½ cups water

2 tablespoons maple syrup, plus more for topping (optional)

1 teaspoon vanilla extract

½ teaspoon ground cinnamon

Pinch salt

½ to 1 cup nondairy milk

2 cups granola (any variety)

2 cups Fresh Fruit Compote (page 146)

Sliced bananas, for topping (optional)

Toasted walnuts, for topping (optional)

1. In your Instant Pot®, combine the quinoa, water, maple syrup, vanilla, cinnamon, and salt. Lock the lid and turn the steam release handle to Sealing. Using the Manual function, set the cooker to High Pressure for 8 minutes (7 minutes at sea level).

2. When the cook time is complete, let the pressure release naturally for 10 minutes; quick release any remaining pressure.

3. Carefully remove the lid and stir the quinoa. Add enough milk to get the desired consistency. Spoon the quinoa mix into bowls and top with granola, compote, and any additional toppings, as desired.

MAKE-AHEAD TIP: The quinoa and compote can be made during your weekly meal prep and stored separately. Simply reheat and assemble for a delicious breakfast!

PER SERVING: Calories: 507; Total fat: 7g; Saturated fat: 2g; Sodium: 100mg; Carbs: 104g; Fiber: 9g; Protein: 10g

HEALTHY-YET-TASTY OATS

GLUTEN FREE • SOY FREE

This is my go-to breakfast on days I know will be challenging. Flavors I enjoy combined with all the vitamins and nutrients (and superfoods!) give me an extra boost and help me feel like I can accomplish anything! It's also nice to have such a healthy breakfast that is easy to make while getting ready in the morning. I've found it helps me make smart food choices that set me up to have a great day. **SERVES 4 TO 6**

PREP TIME:
2 minutes

COOKING SETTING:
Manual, High Pressure for 12 minutes (10 minutes at sea level)

RELEASE:
Natural for 10 minutes, then Quick

TOTAL TIME:
24 minutes

2 cups steel cut oats

4½ cups water

½ to 1 cup nondairy milk

2 tablespoons agave, or maple syrup (optional)

¼ teaspoon salt (optional)

¼ to ½ cup chia seeds

1 cup chopped walnuts

1 cup fresh blueberries

1. In your Instant Pot®, stir together the oats and water. Lock the lid and turn the steam release handle to Sealing. Using the Manual function, set the cooker to High Pressure for 12 minutes (10 minutes at sea level).

2. When the cook time is complete, turn off the Instant Pot®. Let the pressure release naturally for 10 minutes; quick release any remaining pressure.

3. Carefully remove the lid and add the milk. Stir in the agave and salt (if using) and top with the chia seeds, walnuts, and blueberries.

PER SERVING: Calories: 328; Total fat: 13g; Saturated fat: 1g; Sodium: 198mg; Carbs: 47g; Fiber: 11g; Protein: 10g

PREP TIME:
7 minutes

COOKING SETTING:
Sauté Low
for 2 minutes;
Manual, High
Pressure for
18 minutes
(15 minutes at
sea level)

RELEASE:
Natural for
10 minutes,
then Quick

TOTAL TIME:
37 minutes

KALE & SWEET POTATO MINI QUICHE

BUDGET FRIENDLY · NUT FREE

These crustless quiches are great for brunch with friends and are especially tasty when schmeared on vegan-buttered toast! A dash of salt and pepper on top is all you really need, though they're also good with a little avocado or vegan cheese. If you don't want to share, you can definitely keep them all to yourself for weekday breakfasts. After they've cooled, seal them in an airtight container and keep refrigerated for up to 4 days. **MAKES 7 QUICHES**

Nonstick cooking spray, for preparing the mold

1 (14-ounce) package firm tofu, lightly pressed

¼ cup nondairy milk

¼ cup nutritional yeast

1 tablespoon cornstarch

½ to 1 teaspoon kala namak, or sea salt, plus more for seasoning

½ teaspoon garlic powder

½ teaspoon onion powder

½ teaspoon ground turmeric

½ cup shredded sweet potato

Handful kale leaves, chopped small

1 cup plus 1 tablespoon water

Vegan-buttered toast, for serving

Freshly ground black pepper

---

1. Lightly coat an 8¼-inch silicone egg-bites mold with nonstick spray and set aside.

2. In a food processor, combine the tofu, milk, yeast, cornstarch, kala namak, garlic powder, onion powder, and turmeric. Blend until smooth.

3. On your Instant Pot®, select Sauté Low. When the display reads "Hot," add the sweet potato, kale, and 1 tablespoon of water. Sauté for 1 to 2 minutes (you may need to turn off the Instant Pot® if the vegetables start to stick to the bottom, but that's okay because it stays hot). Stir the veggies into the tofu mixture and spoon the mixture into the prepared mold. Cover the mold tightly with aluminum foil and place on a trivet. Add the remaining 1 cup of water to the inner pot and use the trivet's handles to lower the trivet and mold into the pot.

4. Lock the lid and turn the steam release handle to Sealing. Using the Manual function, set the cooker to High Pressure for 18 minutes (15 minutes at sea level).

5. When the cook time is complete, let the pressure release naturally for 10 minutes; quick release any remaining pressure.

6. Carefully remove the lid. Remove the silicone mold from the Instant Pot® and pull off the foil. Leave the mold on the trivet and let cool for a few minutes. The bites will continue to firm as they cool. When ready to eat, schmear the tofu bites onto a piece of vegan-buttered toast and top with a little salt and pepper.

SUBSTITUTION TIP: Use your favorite veggies here! Spinach and tomato is my second favorite combination (squeeze the excess liquid from the tomatoes with a paper towel or the tofu won't firm up all the way).

PER SERVING: Calories: 150; Total fat: 5g; Saturated fat: 1g; Sodium: 46mg; Carbs: 16g; Fiber: 5g; Protein: 14g

PREP TIME:
2 hours

COOKING SETTING:
Manual, High Pressure for 2 minutes; Sauté Low for 8 minutes

RELEASE:
Quick

TOTAL TIME:
2 hours 10 minutes

POBLANO–SWEET POTATO HASH

GLUTEN FREE · NUT FREE

I love poblano peppers—they're not crazy hot, but they have so much smoky flavor. This hash is worth the extra step of preparing the tofu separately (and with different seasonings); when you combine it with the potatoes and peppers, you end up with multiple delicious textures and a more complex flavor. It's also important to take the time to let the liquid press out of the tofu to ensure it can get nice and crispy.
SERVES 4 TO 6

---

2 sweet potatoes, cut into large dice

1 cup water

1 (14-ounce) package extra-firm tofu, pressed for at least 2 hours, crumbled in a food processor

1 teaspoon ground turmeric

½ teaspoon smoked paprika

½ teaspoon kala namak, or sea salt

1 to 2 tablespoons oil

1 small onion, diced

1 bell pepper, any color, diced

2 poblano peppers, roasted, cut into large dice

2 garlic cloves, minced

1½ teaspoons Montreal chicken seasoning

---

1. In your Instant Pot®, combine the sweet potatoes and water. Lock the lid and turn the steam release handle to Sealing. Using the Manual function, set the cooker to High Pressure for 2 minutes.

2. While the sweet potatoes cook, heat a skillet over medium heat on your stovetop. Add the tofu crumbles, turmeric, paprika, and kala namak. Cook for 4 to 5 minutes, stirring often, until the tofu gets a little crispy. Remove from the heat.

3. When the Instant Pot® cook time is complete, quick release the pressure.

4. Carefully remove the lid and pour the contents of the inner pot into a colander or steamer basket to drain. Return the inner pot to the Instant Pot® and set the sweet potatoes aside.

5. On your Instant Pot®, select Sauté Low. When the display reads "Hot," add 1 tablespoon of oil. Heat the oil until it shimmers. Add the onion and bell pepper. Cook for 2 to 3 minutes. Add the poblanos, garlic, and Montreal chicken seasoning and cook for 1 minute more.

6. If the pot looks dry, add the remaining 1 tablespoon of oil. Add the sweet potatoes back to the pot. Cook for 2 to 3 minutes, stirring frequently.

7. Turn off the Instant Pot® and stir in the tofu. Mix well to combine and serve warm.

TECHNIQUE TIP: Some specialty grocers sell poblano peppers already roasted, but it's also easy to roast your own—and it makes your kitchen smell delicious. Rub the peppers with oil and place them on a baking sheet. Roast in a 425°F oven for 30 to 45 minutes, or until the skin is charred on all sides. Using tongs, place the peppers in a bowl and cover it. Let the peppers sit for 15 minutes. Run the roasted pepper under cold water and rub off the skins. Now they're ready to use, eat, or freeze for later.

PER SERVING: Calories: 238; Total fat: 13g; Saturated fat: 2g; Sodium: 420mg; Carbs: 22g; Fiber: 4g; Protein: 12g

PREP TIME:
12 minutes

COOKING SETTING:
Sauté Low for 8 minutes; Manual, High Pressure for 3 minutes

RELEASE:
Quick

TOTAL TIME:
23 minutes

TEMPEH "SAUSAGE"

BUDGET FRIENDLY · NUT FREE

While there are many "mock meats" available these days, a lot of health-conscious vegans avoid them. These products tend to be highly processed and may contain ingredients we can't pronounce. That's why I created this simple "sausage" recipe. It's simply a combination of tempeh and delicious spices! Whip up a batch to have handy for your favorite breakfast dishes, like Breakfast Enchiladas (page 34). **SERVES 4 TO 6**

1 tablespoon olive oil

1 (8-ounce) package unflavored tempeh

2 teaspoons vegan Worcestershire sauce

1½ teaspoons smoked paprika

1 teaspoon onion powder

1 teaspoon garlic powder

1 teaspoon dried sage

½ teaspoon dried oregano

½ teaspoon salt, plus more as needed

¼ teaspoon freshly ground black pepper

Pinch chili powder

1 cup water

1. On your Instant Pot®, select Sauté Low. When the display reads "Hot," add the oil and heat until it begins to shimmer. With your hands, crumble the tempeh into the hot oil and stir to coat. Add the Worcestershire sauce, paprika, onion powder, garlic powder, sage, oregano, salt, pepper, and chili powder. Continue to sauté, stirring as needed, for 6 to 7 minutes more.

2. Turn off the Instant Pot® and add the water. Use your spoon to scrape up any bits of flavor that have stuck to the bottom of the pot. Stir well. Lock the lid and turn the steam release handle to Sealing. Using the Manual function, set the cooker to High Pressure for 3 minutes.

3. When the cook time is complete, quick release the pressure.

4. Carefully remove the lid. Select Sauté Low again and let the remaining liquid cook off. Taste and season with more salt, as needed.

INGREDIENT TIP: Tempeh contains a lot of protein (31 grams per cup) and is loaded with copper, manganese, riboflavin, and niacin.

PER SERVING: Calories: 161; Total fat: 10g; Saturated fat: 2g; Sodium: 325mg; Carbs: 8g; Fiber: 1g; Protein: 12g

SWEET VANILLA POLENTA

BUDGET FRIENDLY · GLUTEN FREE · NUT FREE · SOY FREE

Polenta is more commonly served later in the day, but don't let that stop you from enjoying this first thing in the morning. Brown sugar and vanilla are a perfect pair, especially topped with fresh fruit. If polenta is new to you, all the more reason to try it. I cooked with polenta for the first time when I was a new vegan (veganism leads to experimenting with new ingredients, in my experience) and I instantly fell in love. Now I try to include it as often as possible in both savory and sweet recipes. **SERVES 4**

PREP TIME:
5 minutes

COOKING SETTING:
Porridge for 20 minutes (17 minutes at sea level)

RELEASE:
Natural for 10 to 15 minutes

TOTAL TIME:
40 minutes

1 cup polenta

2 cups water

2 cups nondairy milk, plus more as needed

½ to 1 teaspoon salt, plus more as needed

⅓ cup packed light brown sugar

1½ teaspoons vanilla extract

Fresh fruit, for topping (I like sliced banana or blueberries)

1. In your Instant Pot®, combine the polenta, water, milk, and salt, stirring well to break up any lumps. Lock the lid and turn the steam release handle to Sealing. Using the Porridge function, set the cook time for 20 minutes (17 minutes at sea level).

2. When the cook time is complete, turn off the pressure cooker and let the pressure release naturally until the pin drops, about 10 to 15 minutes.

3. Carefully remove the lid. There will be liquid on top, but once you stir it in, the polenta will be beautifully creamy! Stir in the brown sugar and vanilla. Taste and add another pinch of salt, if you like, as well as more milk if you want it creamier. Top with the fruit and enjoy.

INGREDIENT TIP: Polenta, refrigerated in an airtight container, will keep for several days.

PER SERVING: Calories: 233; Total fat: 2g; Saturated fat: 0g; Sodium: 387mg; Carbs: 50g; Fiber: 2g; Protein: 3g

PREP TIME:
2 minutes

COOKING SETTING:
Manual, High Pressure for 10 minutes (9 minutes at sea level)

RELEASE:
Natural for 10 minutes, then Quick

TOTAL TIME:
22 minutes

MAPLE MORNING MILLET

BUDGET FRIENDLY · GLUTEN FREE · NUT FREE · SOY FREE

If you're not familiar with millet, here is a great recipe to get started. It's a humble grain (often used in birdseed), but when hulled, it's very similar to quinoa and can be used in all sorts of sweet and savory dishes, for all meals of the day. It's also one of the least expensive grains to buy, which appeals to my frugal side. Top it with whatever berries are in season (or on hand!), and if you want to go one step further, crumble some vegan bacon on top. **SERVES 4 TO 6**

1 cup millet

2 cups water

½ teaspoon ground cinnamon

¼ to ½ teaspoon salt

¼ cup maple syrup

½ to 1 cup nondairy milk

Fresh berries, for topping

1. In your Instant Pot®, stir together the millet, water, cinnamon, and salt. Lock the lid and turn the steam release handle to Sealing. Using the Manual function, set the cooker to High Pressure for 10 minutes (9 minutes at sea level).

2. When the cook time is complete, let the pressure release naturally for 10 minutes; quick release any remaining pressure.

3. Carefully remove the lid and stir in the maple syrup and as much milk as you need to get the consistency you prefer (more milk makes it creamier). I usually add an extra sprinkle of salt, too.

4. Top with the berries and serve.

INGREDIENT TIP: As a native New Englander, I always recommend using real maple syrup. The flavor is so much better and it's a lot less processed than the stuff you find on the lower shelves at the grocery store.

PER SERVING: Calories: 251; Total fat: 3g; Saturated fat: 1g; Sodium: 157mg; Carbs: 50g; Fiber: 5g; Protein: 6g

HOLIDAY FRENCH TOAST CASSEROLE

SOY FREE

I highly recommend serving this breakfast on special occasions. French toast casserole is delicious to begin with, but this is extra special with the addition of Bailey's Almande, which is vegan and gives this dish a sweet, nutty flavor. The casserole may seem dry when it first comes out of the Instant Pot®, but, trust me, once you add maple syrup it is irresistible. If you're serving breakfast to the under-21 crowd, substitute nondairy milk for the Bailey's. **SERVES 4 TO 6**

PREP TIME:
5 minutes

COOKING SETTING:
Manual, High Pressure for 25 minutes (21 minutes at sea level)

RELEASE:
Quick

TOTAL TIME:
30 minutes

Nonstick cooking spray, for preparing the bowl

1 cup water

1 large banana, plus more for topping (optional)

¼ cup maple syrup, plus more for serving

¼ cup Bailey's Almande Almond Milk Liqueur

1 teaspoon vanilla extract

¼ teaspoon kala namak, or sea salt

6 cups cubed, stale French bread

Vegan butter, for topping

1. Spray a 7-cup oven-safe glass bowl with nonstick spray and set aside.

2. Pour the water into your Instant Pot® and place a trivet inside the inner pot.

3. In a large bowl, mash the banana with a fork. Stir in the maple syrup, Bailey's, vanilla, and kala namak, making sure the banana is completely mixed in.

4. Quickly toss the bread in the banana mixture, making sure to get even coverage. Transfer to the prepared bowl, cover tightly with aluminum foil, and place the bowl on top of the trivet in the Instant Pot®. Lock the lid and turn the steam release handle to Sealing. Using the Manual function, set the cooker to High Pressure for 25 minutes (21 minutes at sea level).

5. When the cook time is complete, quick release the pressure.

6. Carefully remove the lid. Serve with toppings as desired, and enjoy!

PER SERVING: Calories: 383; Total fat: 3g; Saturated fat: 1g; Sodium: 542mg; Carbs: 77g; Fiber: 3g; Protein: 12g

PREP TIME:
5 minutes

COOKING SETTING:
Manual, High Pressure for 25 minutes (21 minutes at sea level)

RELEASE:
Quick

TOTAL TIME:
30 minutes

BERRY BERRY CINNAMON TOAST CASSEROLE

NUT FREE • SOY FREE

Yes, another French toast casserole because that's just how good it is! This version has a completely different flavor profile from the Holiday French Toast Casserole (page 29), mainly because it uses applesauce as the egg substitute instead of banana. I love the blueberries and strawberries here; they give the dish a bright taste and keep it from feeling heavy. I recommend you top it with lots of vegan butter and maple syrup. **SERVES 4 TO 6**

Nonstick cooking spray, for preparing the bowl

1 cup water

½ cup applesauce

¼ cup maple syrup, plus more for topping

1 teaspoon vanilla extract

1 teaspoon ground cinnamon

¼ teaspoon kala namak, or sea salt

5 cups cubed, stale French bread

1½ cups fresh blueberries and strawberries (halve or quarter the strawberries)

Vegan butter, for topping

1. Spray a 7-cup oven-safe glass bowl with nonstick spray.

2. Pour the water into the Instant Pot® and place a trivet inside the inner pot.

3. In a large bowl, whisk the applesauce, maple syrup, vanilla, cinnamon, and kala namak.

4. Quickly toss the bread and berries in the apple mixture, making sure to get even coverage. Transfer the mixture to the prepared bowl and cover tightly with aluminum foil. Place the bowl on top of the trivet in the Instant Pot®. Lock the lid and turn the steam release handle to Sealing. Using the Manual function, set the cooker to High Pressure for 25 minutes (21 minutes at sea level).

5. When the cook time is complete, quick release the pressure.

6. Carefully remove the lid and serve with desired toppings.

PER SERVING: Calories: 331; Total fat: 2g; Saturated fat: 0g; Sodium: 430mg; Carbs: 70g; Fiber: 4g; Protein: 10g

BLUEBERRY LEMON BLISS BOWLS

GLUTEN FREE • SOY FREE

Blueberry and lemon go together like peas and carrots, which is why I'm pretty certain this breakfast is destined to become one of your favorites. It's definitely one of mine! The sweetness of the blueberries and the slight tartness of the lemon, plus the crunch of the almonds, are nearly breakfast perfection. I like to whip up a big batch while doing my regular Sunday meal prep and parcel it out into individual servings for the week to help my hectic mornings go more smoothly. **SERVES 4 TO 6**

PREP TIME:
2 minutes

COOKING SETTING:
Manual, High Pressure for 10 minutes (9 minutes at sea level)

RELEASE:
Natural for 10 minutes, then Quick

TOTAL TIME:
22 minutes

1 cup millet, rinsed

2¼ cups water

2 tablespoons maple syrup

1 tablespoon freshly squeezed lemon juice

¼ teaspoon ground nutmeg

¼ teaspoon ground cinnamon

¼ to ½ teaspoon salt

1 cup nondairy milk, plus more as needed

1 cup fresh blueberries

½ cup sliced toasted almonds

Zest of ½ lemon

1. In your Instant Pot®, stir together the millet, water, maple syrup, lemon juice, nutmeg, cinnamon, and salt. Lock the lid and turn the steam release handle to Sealing. Using the Manual function, set the cooker to High Pressure for 10 minutes (9 minutes at sea level).

2. When the cook time is complete, let the pressure release naturally for 10 minutes; quick release any remaining pressure.

3. Carefully remove the lid and stir in the milk, adding more if you like a creamier texture.

4. Top with the blueberries, almonds, and lemon zest before serving.

MAKE-AHEAD TIP: If you're planning to enjoy your bliss the next day, don't add the almonds until you're ready to reheat.

PER SERVING: Calories: 317; Total fat: 9g; Saturated fat: 1g; Sodium: 197mg; Carbs: 52g; Fiber: 7g; Protein: 9g

PREP TIME:
30 to
60 minutes

COOKING
SETTING:
Manual, High
Pressure for
52 minutes
(44 minutes
at sea level)

RELEASE:
Quick

TOTAL TIME:
1 hour
30 minutes to
2 hours

SAVORY TOFU & POTATO CASSEROLE

NUT FREE (WITHOUT THE CASHEW SOUR CREAM)

Here's a traditional breakfast casserole with a compassionate twist! This savory casserole is very filling, and between the tempeh and tofu it also provides a lot of protein. It's hearty enough that you can serve it on its own, but I recommend adding some fresh fruit. And maybe some breakfast potatoes, because really, you can never have enough potatoes. I always enjoy mine with a liberal splash of hot sauce. **SERVES 4 TO 6**

Nonstick cooking spray, for preparing the pan

2 cups frozen hash browns, thawed

Salt

¼ teaspoon freshly ground black pepper, plus more for seasoning

1 (14-ounce) package firm tofu, pressed for 30 to 60 minutes

⅓ cup nutritional yeast

¼ cup nondairy milk

1 teaspoon kala namak, or sea salt

1 teaspoon onion powder

1 teaspoon garlic powder

1 teaspoon ground cumin

½ teaspoon dried oregano

1 batch Tempeh "Sausage" (page 26)

1 cup water

Hot sauce, for serving

Sliced scallion, green and light green parts, for serving

Garden Salsa (page 159), for serving

Cashew Sour Cream (page 160), for serving

1. Lightly coat the bottom of a 7-inch springform pan with nonstick spray and set aside.

2. In a large bowl, toss the hash browns with salt to taste and pepper and set aside.

3. In a food processor, combine the tofu, yeast, milk, kala namak, onion powder, garlic powder, cumin, and oregano. Blend until smooth.

4. Add the tempeh sausage to the hash browns along with one-fourth of the tofu mixture. Stir to combine. Layer this mixture on the bottom of the prepared pan. Top with the remaining tofu mixture. Cover the pan with a paper towel and wrap it tightly in aluminum foil.

5. Pour the water into your Instant Pot® and place a trivet inside the inner pot. Put the springform pan on the trivet. Lock the lid and turn the steam release handle to Sealing. Using the Manual function, set the cooker to High Pressure for 52 minutes (44 minutes at sea level).

6. When the cook time is complete, quick release the pressure.

7. Carefully remove the lid and remove the pan from the Instant Pot®. Take off the foil and paper towel. Let cool before releasing the sides of the pan. Serve topped as desired.

PER SERVING: Calories: 494; Total fat: 25g; Saturated fat: 5g; Sodium: 1043mg; Carbs: 44g; Fiber: 8g; Protein: 29g

PREP TIME:
45 minutes
to 1 hour

COOKING
SETTING:
Sauté Low
for 8 to
10 minutes;
Manual, High
Pressure for
2 minutes

RELEASE:
Quick

TOTAL TIME:
1 hour
12 minutes

BREAKFAST ENCHILADAS

NUT FREE

Mexican food is my favorite, even though I often stray from the traditional ingredients (and I tend to favor flour tortillas no matter what the recipe calls for). Being vegan necessitates even more (slight) conversions, and that's okay! It's our chance to make dishes we love even better. If you're a fan of store-bought vegan cheese, add it to the top before baking (and remove the aluminum foil for the last 5 minutes). Or make your own Cashew Sour Cream (page 160) and Poblano Cheeze Sauce (page 158). **SERVES 8 TO 10**

FOR THE TOFU SCRAMBLE

1 (14-ounce) package firm tofu, pressed for 30 to 60 minutes

½ teaspoon kala namak, or sea salt

½ teaspoon ground turmeric

1 to 2 tablespoons olive oil

1 small onion, cut into large dice

1 bell pepper, any color, cut into large dice

1 jalapeño pepper, diced

2 garlic cloves, minced

1 medium or large tomato, diced

¼ cup nutritional yeast

1 teaspoon ground cumin

½ teaspoon dried oregano

Few pinches red pepper flakes

Salt

Freshly ground black pepper

FOR THE ENCHILADAS

Nonstick cooking spray, for preparing the baking dish

1 batch Tempeh "Sausage" (page 26)

12 (6-inch) tortillas, or 10 (8-inch)

About 1¼ cups Red Hot Enchilada Sauce (page 157), or 1 (10-ounce) can red enchilada sauce

3 or 4 scallions, green and light green parts, sliced

TO MAKE THE TOFU SCRAMBLE

1. In a small bowl (or in your tofu press), use a fork to crumble the tofu. Stir in the kala namak and turmeric. Set aside.

2. On your Instant Pot®, select Sauté Low. When the display reads "Hot," add the oil and heat until it shimmers. Add the onion, bell

pepper, and jalapeño. Cook for 2 to 3 minutes, stirring frequently. Turn off the Instant Pot® and add the garlic. The inner pot will still be hot. Let the veggies cook for another minute or so. Stir in the tomatoes, tofu mixture, nutritional yeast, cumin, oregano, and red pepper flakes. Season to taste with salt and pepper. Lock the lid and turn the steam release handle to Sealing. Using the Manual function, set the cooker to High Pressure for 2 minutes.

3. When the cook time is complete, quick release the pressure.

4. Carefully remove the lid. Select Sauté Low again and cook off the remaining liquid, 3 to 5 minutes, stirring frequently. Taste and adjust the seasonings as desired.

TO MAKE THE ENCHILADAS

1. Preheat the oven to 375°F. Spray the bottom of a 9-by-13-inch glass baking dish with nonstick spray.

2. To build your enchiladas, add 1 spoonful of tempeh sausage to a tortilla, followed by 2 to 3 spoonfuls of tofu scramble (depending on the size of the tortillas), and roll tightly. Place in the prepared baking dish, seam-side down. Repeat for the remaining tortillas.

3. Spoon about two-thirds of the enchilada sauce over the top and sprinkle on the scallions. Cover the dish with aluminum foil and bake for 20 minutes (18 minutes at sea level).

4. Top as desired before serving.

PER SERVING: Calories: 528; Total fat: 25g; Saturated fat: 4g; Sodium: 705mg; Carbs: 55g; Fiber: 11g; Protein: 30g

PREP TIME:
15 minutes

COOKING SETTING:
Stovetop for 5 minutes; Manual, High Pressure for 12 minutes (10 minutes at sea level)

RELEASE:
Natural for 10 minutes, then Quick

TOTAL TIME:
42 minutes

STRAWBERRY OATS WITH MAPLE-TOASTED WALNUTS

GLUTEN FREE · SOY FREE

You may as well go ahead and double the amount of maple-toasted walnuts because, if you're anything like me, you won't be able to stop snacking on them! In fact, they can be made ahead and refrigerated in an airtight container. Add them to your breakfast oats (or lunch salads . . . or snack. Who's counting?) throughout the week. **SERVES 4 TO 6**

FOR THE MAPLE-TOASTED WALNUTS

3 cups walnut halves

½ cup maple syrup

½ teaspoon salt

FOR THE OATS

2 cups steel cut oats

2½ cups water

2½ cups unsweetened nondairy milk, divided

2 teaspoons vanilla extract

¼ teaspoon salt

2 cups strawberries, chopped or sliced

½ cup packed light brown sugar

TO MAKE THE MAPLE-TOASTED WALNUTS

1. Cover a heat-resistant flat surface with parchment paper.

2. On your stovetop, heat a skillet over medium-high heat. Add the walnuts, maple syrup, and salt. Cook for 3 to 4 minutes, stirring frequently, or until the maple syrup has caramelized and the walnuts are toasted. Pour the mixture onto the parchment-covered surface, spreading it out so it doesn't clump into one large piece. Let cool. Break into bite-size pieces.

TO MAKE THE OATS

1. In your Instant Pot®, combine the oats, water, 2 cups of milk, the vanilla, and salt. Stir well.

2. Lock the lid and turn the steam release handle to Sealing. Using the Manual function, set the cooker to High Pressure for 12 minutes (10 minutes at sea level).

3. When the cook time is complete, turn off the Instant Pot®. Let the pressure release naturally for 10 minutes; quick release any remaining pressure.

4. Carefully remove the lid and stir in the remaining ½ cup of milk, the strawberries, and brown sugar. Top individual servings with the toasted walnuts.

INGREDIENT TIP: Did you know walnuts have been proven to improve brain health? They also act as a mood booster, which make them a great part of any breakfast!

PER SERVING: Calories: 542; Total fat: 20g; Saturated fat: 2g; Sodium: 483mg; Carbs: 82g; Fiber: 9g; Protein: 10g

Lemon Ginger
Asparagus

4

APPETIZERS, STARTERS & SIDES

PREP TIME:
3 minutes

COOKING
SETTING:
Manual, High
Pressure for
2 minutes

RELEASE:
Quick

TOTAL TIME:
5 minutes

CANDIED CARROTS

BUDGET FRIENDLY · GLUTEN FREE · NUT FREE · SOY FREE

My mom didn't cook much when I was young (She was busy! Kids + dogs + cats + owning her own business = little time to cook), but she made a few dishes I remember fondly, and this is one. The sweet and salty combination guarantees these carrots will be a hit with pretty much everyone, and they're quick and easy to prepare as part of a larger meal. I know some people consider this dish to be just for holiday meals, but I say it's good year-round. **SERVES 4 TO 6**

---

1 (1-pound) bag baby carrots

1 cup water

3 tablespoons vegan butter

3 tablespoons packed light brown sugar

½ to 1 teaspoon salt

---

1. Put the carrots in a steamer basket and place the basket into the Instant Pot®. Pour in the water. Lock the lid and turn the steam release handle to Sealing. Using the Manual function, set the cooker to High Pressure for 2 minutes.

2. When the cook time is complete, quick release the pressure.

3. Carefully remove the lid and add the butter, letting it melt into the carrots for 1 minute or so.

4. Add the brown sugar and salt. Stir, stir, stir until the carrots are coated. Taste and add a touch more salt, if you'd like.

INGREDIENT TIP: Both light and dark brown sugars are made with sugar and molasses. Dark brown sugar has more molasses and, therefore, a stronger flavor. I tend to use light brown sugar, but both are delicious and can be substituted for each other.

PER SERVING: Calories: 123; Total fat: 7g; Saturated fat: 1g; Sodium: 354mg; Carbs: 16g; Fiber: 3g; Protein: 1g

ANYTHING-BUT-BASIC BAKED POTATOES

BUDGET FRIENDLY · GLUTEN FREE · NUT FREE · SOY FREE

Baked potatoes are a wonderful side dish to so many meals, but baking them in the oven takes forever. And, during the warmer months, who wants the oven on for that long anyway? Microwaving is an option, but the texture is never as good as baked. Solution? Pressure cooking your spuds gives you all that wonderful fluffy texture without heating up your kitchen. It's a potato miracle! **SERVES 4**

4 medium russet potatoes, scrubbed well, pierced on all sides with a fork

1 cup water

Toppings, as desired

PREP TIME:
5 minutes

COOKING SETTING:
Manual, High Pressure for 15 minutes (13 minutes at sea level)

RELEASE:
Natural for 15 minutes, then Quick

TOTAL TIME:
35 minutes

1. Add the water and a trivet to the Instant Pot®. Place the potatoes on the trivet. Lock the lid and turn the steam release handle to Sealing. Using the Manual function, set the cooker to High Pressure for 15 minutes (13 minutes at sea level).

2. When the cook time is complete, let the Instant Pot® go into Keep Warm mode and let the pressure release naturally for 15 minutes; quick release any remaining pressure.

3. Add toppings and ta-da!

PER SERVING: Calories: 147; Total fat: 0g; Saturated fat: 0g; Sodium: 13mg; Carbs: 34g; Fiber: 5g; Protein: 4g

PREP TIME:
5 minutes

**COOKING
SETTING:**
Low Pressure
for 0 minutes

RELEASE:
Quick

TOTAL TIME:
5 minutes

LEMON GINGER ASPARAGUS

BUDGET FRIENDLY • GLUTEN FREE • NUT FREE • SOY FREE

This dish just screams SPRINGTIME to me! The light, bright flavors along with one of my very favorite vegetables create a delicious side dish. You'll notice I've listed a range of measurements for the seasonings. That's because ginger and lemon can quickly overwhelm the asparagus if you're not careful. I recommend starting with ½ teaspoon of each and tasting after adding the asparagus. It's easy to add more, but there's no turning back if you add too much. **SERVES 4 TO 6**

1 bunch asparagus, tough ends removed, halved if remaining pieces are longer than 4 inches

1 cup water

2 tablespoons olive oil

1½ teaspoons to 1 tablespoon freshly squeezed lemon juice

½ to 1 teaspoon salt

½ to ¾ teaspoon grated peeled fresh ginger

1. Place the asparagus in a steamer basket and put the basket into the Instant Pot®. Add the water. Lock the lid and turn the steam release handle to Sealing. Using the Manual function, set the cooker to Low Pressure for 0 minutes.

2. When the cook time is complete, quick release the pressure.

3. In a serving bowl, stir together the oil, lemon juice, ½ teaspoon of salt, and ½ teaspoon of ginger.

4. Carefully remove the lid and add the asparagus to the bowl. Toss to combine. Taste and add the remaining lemon juice and/or ginger, as needed.

PER SERVING: Calories: 84; Total fat: 7g; Saturated fat: 1g; Sodium: 294mg; Carbs: 5g; Fiber: 2g; Protein: 3g

"ROASTED" GARLIC

BUDGET FRIENDLY · GLUTEN FREE (WITHOUT THE BREAD) ·
NUT FREE · SOY FREE

This is a recreation of my all-time favorite appetizer in Italian
restaurants. It's so simple—all you do is schmear the roasted garlic
on slices of crusty bread. If you're feeling fancy you could drizzle a
little olive oil on the bread, and perhaps a sprinkle of salt and pepper.
Either way it's definitely delicious—but not recommended for a first
date! **SERVES 4**

1 cup water

**4 large heads garlic, tops cut
off to expose just the top
of each clove**

**Olive oil (I recommend
butter-infused)**

Crusty bread, for serving

1. Add the water and a trivet to the Instant Pot®. Place the garlic on the
trivet, cut-side up. Lock the lid and turn the steam release handle to
Sealing. Using the Manual function, set the cooker to High Pressure for
6 minutes (5 minutes at sea level).

2. When the cook time is complete, turn off the cooker and let the
pressure release naturally until the pin drops, about 10 minutes.

3. Carefully remove the lid. Using tongs, transfer the garlic to a baking
sheet or other heatproof dish. Generously drizzle with olive oil, making
sure all the garlic gets oiled! Broil on low for about 5 minutes. Watch so
it doesn't burn, but you want it to be golden and caramelized. Remove
from the oven and let cool for at least 10 minutes.

4. Serve immediately, plated in the skins as is (that's how it's done in
restaurants). Your guests can use their butter knives to scoop out the
cloves for schmearing.

*PER SERVING: Calories: 408; Total fat: 26g; Saturated fat: 4g; Sodium: 318mg;
Carbs: 39g; Fiber: 2g; Protein: 8g*

PREP TIME:
5 minutes

**COOKING
SETTING:**
Manual, High
Pressure for
6 minutes
(5 minutes
at sea level);
broiler for
5 minutes

RELEASE:
Natural for
10 minutes

TOTAL TIME:
26 minutes

PREP TIME:
5 minutes

COOKING SETTING:
Manual, High Pressure for 10 minutes (9 minutes at sea level)

RELEASE:
Quick

TOTAL TIME:
15 minutes

STEAMED ARTICHOKES

GLUTEN FREE · NUT FREE · SOY FREE

Artichokes may seem scary at first, but I promise they're worth the time and effort. In the name of research (and my love of eating artichokes) I've made them all kinds of ways: grilled, boiled, and roasted. In my experience, the quickest and easiest way to make them is in the Instant Pot®. They cook quickly and perfectly, and all that's left to do is dip the leaves, one by one, into a delicious sauce! **SERVES 2 TO 4**

4 or 5 artichokes, rinsed

1 large lemon

1 cup water

2 garlic cloves, peeled

1. With a sharp knife, cut about 1 inch off the top (petal end) of one artichoke. Remove the tough outer leaves (usually one or two layers), and trim off the stem. Repeat with the remaining artichokes.

2. Cut most of the lemon into ¼-inch-thick round slices, leaving one end. Cut that end into wedges. Rub the lemon wedges over the entire outside of the artichokes, focusing on the cut edges. This keeps them from browning and adds extra flavor.

3. In your Instant Pot®, combine the water, lemon slices, and garlic. Place a trivet into the pot and put the artichokes on the trivet in a single layer, stem-side down. Lock the lid and turn the steam release handle to Sealing. Using the Manual function, set the cooker to High Pressure for 10 minutes (9 minutes at sea level).

4. When the cook time is complete, quick release the pressure.

5. Carefully remove the lid. Using tongs, remove the artichokes and serve warm. Enjoy by dipping each leaf in your favorite dipping sauce and pulling out the artichoke meat with your teeth.

SERVING TIP: Artichokes are delicious on their own, but let's be real—the dip matters! You can change it up according to your mood or the season, but my go-to is champagne vinaigrette. Try salad dressing or even the Poblano Cheeze Sauce (page 158)!

PER SERVING: Calories: 165; Total fat: 1g; Saturated fat: 0g; Sodium: 306mg; Carbs: 38g; Fiber: 18g; Protein: 11g

GARLICKY LEMON BROCCOLI

BUDGET FRIENDLY • GLUTEN FREE • NUT FREE • SOY FREE

This broccoli is a healthy side dish with a mild flavor that lets your main dish shine. Sometimes simple is best! And broccoli is always a winner in my book. Did you know broccoli was first cultivated in Italy during ancient Roman times, becoming common in England and America in the 1700s? I can imagine the pilgrims eating broccoli, but I'm sure theirs wasn't prepared with lemon or garlic! Those poor pilgrims never knew what they were missing. **SERVES 2 TO 4**

PREP TIME:
5 minutes

COOKING SETTING:
Manual, High Pressure for 0 minutes

RELEASE:
Quick

TOTAL TIME:
5 minutes

1 cup water

4 garlic cloves, roughly chopped

6 cups chopped broccoli

Juice of 1 lemon

½ to 1 teaspoon salt

Zest of 1 lemon

1. In your Instant Pot®, combine the water and garlic. Place the broccoli in a steamer basket and put the basket into the inner pot. Pour the lemon juice over the broccoli so it runs down into the water. Lock the lid and turn the steam release handle to Sealing. Using the Manual function, set the cooker to High Pressure for 0 minutes.

2. When the cook time is complete, quick release the pressure.

3. Carefully remove the lid and remove the broccoli. Sprinkle the salt and lemon zest over the broccoli. Stir well.

PER SERVING: Calories: 108; Total fat: 1g; Saturated fat: 0g; Sodium: 453mg; Carbs: 21g; Fiber: 7g; Protein: 8g

PREP TIME:
15 minutes

COOKING
SETTING:
Oven for 5 to
6 minutes;
Steam for
2 minutes

RELEASE:
None

TOTAL TIME:
23 minutes

SWEET POTATO SLAW IN WONTON CUPS

NUT FREE

These little "slaw cups" make a light, fun appetizer for any party. They're also full of nutrients! Sweet potatoes are high in fiber, as well as vitamins A and C. Cabbage (which is an overlooked veggie, in my opinion) offers lots of vitamin B_6 and K. As a cruciferous vegetable, it is also believed to help lower your risk of cancer! The one thing these cups don't do is hold up well to reheating, so I recommend preparing them right before serving. **MAKES 12 TO 15 CUPS**

Nonstick cooking spray, for preparing the muffin tin

12 to 15 wonton or dumpling wrappers

1 cup water

2 cups sliced green cabbage (roughly 1 small head)

1 cup shredded sweet potato

½ sweet onion, sliced

2 tablespoons lite soy sauce

1 tablespoon hoisin sauce

1½ tablespoons freshly squeezed lime juice

1½ teaspoons sesame oil

Zest of 1 lime

½ teaspoon ground ginger, plus more to taste

3 scallions, green and light green parts, sliced

1. Preheat the oven to 350°F. Lightly coat a muffin tin with the nonstick spray.

2. Place one wonton wrapper in each well of the prepared tin, pressing down to create a cup shape. Bake for 5 to 6 minutes, or until the cups are crispy and lightly browned. Set aside to cool.

3. Pour the water into your Instant Pot®. Place the cabbage, sweet potato, and onion into a steamer basket and put the basket on a trivet. Lock the lid in place. Select Steam and set the cook time for 2 minutes. Because the Steam function doesn't seal the Instant Pot®, there's no need to turn the steam release handle to Sealing or release any pressure.

4. While the veggies steam, in a medium bowl, stir together the soy sauce, hoisin sauce, lime juice, oil, lime zest, and ginger.

5. When the cook time is complete, carefully remove the lid and stir in the veggies, making sure all are coated with the sauce. Taste and add more ginger, if desired.

6. When ready to serve, fill the cups with the slaw and sprinkle the tops with scallion. Enjoy warm or at room temperature.

SUBSTITUTION TIP: If you don't want to make your own wonton cups, premade fillo cups work well and are available at most grocery stores.

PER SERVING (2 AS AN APPETIZER): Calories: 344; Total fat: 5g; Saturated fat: 1g; Sodium: 1455mg; Carbs: 65g; Fiber: 8g; Protein: 11g

PREP TIME:
5 minutes

COOKING
SETTING:
Manual, High
Pressure for
20 minutes
(17 minutes at
sea level)

RELEASE:
Quick

TOTAL TIME:
25 minutes

ALWAYS PERFECT BEETS

BUDGET FRIENDLY · GLUTEN FREE · NUT FREE · SOY FREE

Beets are so easy to make in the Instant Pot®, and ideal for salads, snacking, or as a side dish. I use them regularly in smoothies and to make the prettiest pink Ginger Beet Hummus (page 50). Sometimes I enjoy them with just a sprinkle of sea salt. **SERVES 4 TO 6**

6 beets, roughly 6 inches in circumference, leafy greens (if attached) and roots trimmed

1 cup water

1. Scrub the beets under cold running water. The skin will be thick and bumpy in parts; just make sure all the dirt is gone.

2. Add the water to your Instant Pot® and place a steamer basket inside. Place the beets in the basket in a single layer (or with as little overlap as possible). Seal and lock the lid and turn the steam release handle to Sealing. Using the Manual function, set the cooker to High Pressure for 20 minutes (17 minutes at sea level).

3. When the cook time is complete, quick release the pressure.

4. Carefully remove the lid. Using tongs, remove the beets. I don't peel mine, but if you want to, simply place them in a colander and rub the skins while running them under cold water. Cut them into quarters and season as desired.

INGREDIENT TIP: If cooking larger beets, the rule of thumb is 2 to 3 minutes more at High Pressure for every ½-inch increase in circumference.

PER SERVING: Calories: 66; Total fat: 0g; Saturated fat: 0g; Sodium: 116mg; Carbs: 15g; Fiber: 3g; Protein: 3g

CREAMY CORN

GLUTEN FREE • SOY FREE

Growing up, creamed corn might have been my favorite vegetable. Never homemade though—it had to be from a can. I was a big fan of foods that came from cans! As I've gotten older and my taste buds have matured, I've learned to appreciate the benefits of making my own from scratch, and playing with the flavor. My favorite addition is definitely smoked paprika—it makes it taste like you snuck a little bacon in there! **SERVES 4 TO 6**

PREP TIME:
5 minutes

COOKING SETTING:
Slow Cooker mode for 20 minutes

RELEASE:
None

TOTAL TIME:
25 minutes

1 cup raw cashews, soaked in water overnight, drained, and rinsed well

1 cup DIY Vegetable Stock (page 154), or store-bought stock

2 tablespoons freshly squeezed lemon juice

1 tablespoon sugar

1 teaspoon salt, plus more for seasoning

½ teaspoon vegetable oil

20 ounces frozen sweet corn

¾ cup nondairy milk

1 tablespoon vegan butter

¼ teaspoon smoked paprika

Freshly ground black pepper

1. In a blender or food processor, combine the cashews, stock, lemon juice, sugar, salt, and oil. Blend until smooth. Pour the cashew mixture into the Instant Pot®. Add the corn, milk, butter, and paprika. Season to taste with salt and pepper. Select Slow Cooker mode and set the cook time for 20 minutes. Cover the cooker with a tempered glass lid (see page 6).

2. When the cook time is complete, carefully remove the lid and stir the creamed corn. If there's too much liquid, select Sauté Normal and cook for 1 to 2 minutes to reduce it (be careful of spatter!).

PER SERVING: Calories: 395; Total fat: 23g; Saturated fat: 4g; Sodium: 643mg; Carbs: 44g; Fiber: 3g; Protein: 12g

PREP TIME:
5 minutes

COOKING SETTING:
Manual, High Pressure for 20 minutes (17 minutes at sea level)

RELEASE:
Quick

TOTAL TIME:
25 minutes

GINGER BEET HUMMUS

BUDGET FRIENDLY · GLUTEN FREE · NUT FREE · SOY FREE

Homemade hummus is easy and fun to make. I love making it with beets, but I've also been known to go a little crazy with garlic, jalapeños, and black beans. It's also fun to save money, and we all know how pricey that fancy store-bought hummus can be. Most store brands also contain a lot of oil, if that's something you're concerned about. Making your own means you control the ingredients. Now all you have to do is decide between celery sticks and pita bread for dipping! **SERVES 4 TO 6**

2 beets, leafy greens (if attached) and roots trimmed

1 cup water

1 (15-ounce) can chickpeas, drained, liquid reserved

Juice of 1 lemon

½-inch piece fresh ginger, peeled

2 teaspoons tahini

1 teaspoon salt

½ teaspoon garlic powder

Zest of 1 lemon

1. Scrub the beets under cold running water. The skin will be thick and bumpy in parts; just make sure all the dirt is gone.

2. In your Instant Pot®, combine the beets and water. Lock the lid and turn the steam release handle to Sealing. Using the Manual function, set the cooker to High Pressure for 20 minutes (17 minutes at sea level).

3. When the cook time is complete, quick release the pressure.

4. Carefully remove the lid. Using tongs, remove the beets and run them under cold water, rubbing vigorously to remove the skins.

5. Quarter 1½ of the beets and add them to a food processor along with the chickpeas, lemon juice, ginger, tahini, salt, and garlic powder. Blend until completely smooth, adding the reserved chickpea liquid, as needed, to get a smooth, creamy texture (I usually use most of it). Transfer to a serving bowl.

6. Dice the remaining ½ beet and sprinkle it over the hummus, followed by the lemon zest.

> **SUBSTITUTION TIP:** If you don't like the flavor of tahini, or don't have any on hand, substitute 2 teaspoons of sesame oil or nut butter (cashew, almond, or sunflower butter work best).

PER SERVING: Calories: 159; Total fat: 3g; Saturated fat: 0g; Sodium: 645mg; Carbs: 29g; Fiber: 6g; Protein: 6g

Mom's
Corn Chowder

5

SOUPS, STEWS &
CHILIS

**COOKING
SETTING:**
Manual, High
Pressure for
4 minutes
(3 minutes at
sea level)

VEGGIE NOODLE SOUP

BUDGET FRIENDLY • NUT FREE • SOY FREE

This soup is delicious, healthy, easy to make, and guaranteed to cure the common cold (well, maybe not that last part, but it can't hurt). It's also great for cleaning out your crisper and pantry, and even if you have to head to the store, it's an inexpensive trip—proof that good meals don't always require fancy ingredients! **SERVES 4 TO 6**

4 celery stalks, chopped into bite-size pieces

4 carrots, chopped into bite-size pieces

2 sweet potatoes, peeled and chopped into bite-size pieces

1 sweet onion, chopped into bite-size pieces

1 cup broccoli florets

1 tomato, diced

2 garlic cloves, minced

1 bay leaf

1 teaspoon dried oregano

1 teaspoon dried thyme

1 teaspoon dried basil

1 to 2 teaspoons salt

Pinch freshly ground black pepper

1 cup dried pasta (I prefer a small pasta shape)

4 cups DIY Vegetable Stock (page 154), or store-bought stock, plus more as needed

1 to 1½ cups water, plus more as needed

Chopped fresh parsley, for garnishing (optional)

Lemon zest, for garnishing (optional)

Crackers, for serving (optional)

1. In your Instant Pot®, combine the celery, carrots, sweet potatoes, onion, broccoli, tomato, garlic, bay leaf, oregano, thyme, basil, salt, pepper, pasta, stock, and water, making sure all the good stuff is submerged (add more water or stock, if needed). Lock the lid and turn the steam release handle to Sealing. Using the Manual function, set the cooker to High Pressure for 4 minutes (3 minutes at sea level).

2. When the cook time is complete, let the pressure release naturally for 5 minutes; quick release any remaining pressure.

3. Carefully remove the lid and stir the soup. Remove and discard the bay leaf and enjoy garnished as desired!

PER SERVING: Calories: 197; Total fat: 3g; Saturated fat: 2g; Sodium: 754mg; Carbs: 43g; Fiber: 6g; Protein: 6g

CARROT GINGER SOUP

BUDGET FRIENDLY · GLUTEN FREE · NUT FREE · SOY FREE

There are many dishes for which I'll gladly rely on the ground ginger in my pantry to provide that instantly recognizable unique and zesty taste. This soup is not one of them. Fresh ginger is what makes the flavor really come alive, with its hot-yet-sweet bite. It pairs so well with the fresh, mildly sweet carrot, you'll be wondering why we don't use this combination more often. **SERVES 2 TO 3**

PREP TIME:
10 minutes

COOKING SETTING:
Manual, High Pressure for 4 minutes (3 minutes at sea level)

RELEASE:
Natural for 5 minutes, then Quick

TOTAL TIME:
19 minutes

7 carrots, chopped

1-inch piece fresh ginger, peeled and chopped

½ sweet onion, chopped

1¼ cups DIY Vegetable Stock (page 154), or store-bought stock

½ teaspoon salt, plus more as needed

½ teaspoon sweet paprika

Freshly ground black pepper

Cashew Sour Cream (page 160), for garnishing (optional)

Fresh herbs, for garnishing (optional)

1. In your Instant Pot®, combine the carrots, ginger, onion, stock, salt, and paprika. Season to taste with pepper. Lock the lid and turn the steam release handle to Sealing. Using the Manual function, set the cooker to High Pressure for 4 minutes (3 minutes at sea level).

2. When the cook time is complete, let the pressure release naturally for 5 minutes; quick release any remaining pressure.

3. Carefully remove the lid. Using an immersion blender, blend the soup until completely smooth. Taste and season with more salt and pepper, as needed. Serve with garnishes of choice.

PER SERVING: Calories: 112; Total fat: 1g; Saturated fat: 1g; Sodium: 743mg; Carbs: 26g; Fiber: 6g; Protein: 2g

PREP TIME:
5 minutes

COOKING
SETTING:
Sauté Low for
8 minutes;
Manual, High
Pressure for
5 minutes
(4 minutes at
sea level)

RELEASE:
Natural
release
for 5 to
10 minutes,
then Quick

TOTAL TIME:
28 minutes

CREAMY TOMATO BASIL SOUP

GLUTEN FREE · SOY FREE

A lot of people equate soup with winter, but when it comes to fresh tomatoes and basil, I always think summer. I'm not much of a gardener, but tomatoes and basil are the two plants I can reliably keep alive, so I can just pop outside and pick my ingredients. Try pairing this soup with a grilled vegan cheese sandwich. **SERVES 4 TO 6**

2 tablespoons vegan butter

1 small sweet onion, chopped

2 garlic cloves, minced

1 large carrot, chopped

1 celery stalk, chopped

3 cups DIY Vegetable Stock (page 154), or store-bought stock

3 pounds tomatoes, quartered

¼ cup fresh basil, chopped, plus more for garnishing

¼ cup nutritional yeast

Salt

Freshly ground black pepper

½ to 1 cup nondairy milk (I like cashew or coconut for this)

1. On your Instant Pot®, select Sauté Low. When the display reads "Hot," add the butter to melt. Add the onion and garlic. Sauté for 3 to 4 minutes, stirring frequently. Add the carrot and celery and cook for 1 to 2 minutes more. Continue to stir frequently so nothing sticks.

2. Stir in the stock (now is your chance to reincorporate any veggies stuck to the bottom).

3. Add the tomatoes, basil, yeast, and a pinch or two of salt. Stir one last time. Lock the lid and turn the steam release handle to Sealing. Using the Manual function, set the cooker to High Pressure for 5 minutes (4 minutes at sea level).

4. When the cook time is complete, let the pressure release naturally for 5 to 10 minutes; quick release any remaining pressure.

5. Carefully remove the lid. Using an immersion blender, blend the soup to your preferred consistency. Stir in the milk. Taste and season with salt and pepper, as needed. Garnish with the remaining fresh basil.

PER SERVING: Calories: 186; Total fat: 9g; Saturated fat: 3g; Sodium: 510mg; Carbs: 25g; Fiber: 8g; Protein: 9g

CREAM OF MUSHROOM SOUP

GLUTEN FREE • NUT FREE

I sat through many a Thanksgiving dinner unable to enjoy my beloved green bean casserole thanks to the cream of mushroom soup. Now, though, I'm able to make this creamy soup so quickly and easily that it isn't even reserved for special occasions. It's especially delicious on cold winter days, served with hot crusty bread. **SERVES 4 TO 6**

PREP TIME:
9 minutes

COOKING SETTING:
Sauté Low for 5 minutes; Manual, High Pressure for 6 minutes (5 minutes at sea level)

RELEASE:
Natural release for 10 minutes, then Quick

TOTAL TIME:
30 minutes

2 tablespoons vegan butter

1 small sweet onion, chopped

1½ pounds white button mushrooms, sliced

2 garlic cloves, minced

2 teaspoons dried thyme

1 teaspoon sea salt

1¾ cups DIY Vegetable Stock (page 154), or store-bought stock

½ cup silken tofu

Chopped fresh thyme, for garnishing (optional)

1. On your Instant Pot®, select Sauté Low. When the display reads "Hot," add the butter to melt. Add the onion. Sauté for 1 to 2 minutes. Add the mushrooms, garlic, dried thyme, and salt. Cook for 2 minutes more and then turn off the Instant Pot®.

2. Stir in the stock. Lock the lid and turn the steam release handle to Sealing. Using the Manual function, set the cooker to High pressure for 6 minutes (5 minutes at sea level).

3. While the soup cooks, place the tofu in a food processor or blender and process until smooth. Set aside.

4. When the cook time is complete, let the pressure release naturally for 10 minutes; quick release any remaining pressure.

5. Carefully remove the lid. Using an immersion blender, blend the soup until completely creamy. Stir in the tofu, garnish as desired, and it's ready!

INGREDIENT TIP: Don't waste the rest of that tofu! Simply seal it tightly in a food storage bag and freeze, then add it to your next tofu scramble.

PER SERVING: Calories: 111; Total fat: 8g; Saturated fat: 3g; Sodium: 629mg; Carbs: 10g; Fiber: 2g; Protein: 7g

PREP TIME:
5 minutes

COOKING
SETTING:
Sauté Low
for 5 minutes;
Manual, High
Pressure for
18 minutes
(15 minutes at
sea level)

RELEASE:
Natural
release for
15 minutes,
then Quick

TOTAL TIME:
43 minutes

SPLIT PEA SOUP

BUDGET FRIENDLY · GLUTEN FREE · SOY FREE

I had split pea soup exactly once in my life prior to this year. I was five, and playing at the home of some elderly neighbors. (We lived in a very rural area, and my only friends were elderly neighbors, but I digress.) This lovely woman offered me a bowl of soup, which I refused after one bite because it was: a) Green, and b) Not chicken noodle soup from a can. I'm sure her homemade split pea soup was delicious, but my refusal to eat it lasted another 35 years. Now I'm a convert and recommend it to everyone! The smoked paprika makes it extra tasty, and you won't miss the ham at all. **SERVES 4 TO 6**

1 tablespoon roasted walnut oil

2 carrots, diced

1 celery stalk, diced

1 teaspoon dried thyme

1 teaspoon smoked paprika

1 bay leaf

½ to 1 teaspoon salt,
plus more as needed

2 garlic cloves, minced

1 cup green split peas

2½ cups DIY Vegetable
Stock (page 154), or
store-bought stock

Freshly ground black pepper

1. On your Instant Pot®, select Sauté Low. When the display reads "Hot," add the oil and heat until it shimmers. Add the carrots, celery, thyme, paprika, bay leaf, and salt. Cook for 2 to 3 minutes, stirring frequently, until fragrant. Turn off the Instant Pot® and add the garlic. Cook for 30 seconds.

2. Stir in the split peas and stock. Lock the lid and turn the steam release handle to Sealing. Using the Manual function, set the cooker to High Pressure for 18 minutes (15 minutes at sea level).

3. When the cook time is complete, let the Instant Pot® go into Keep Warm mode and let the pressure release naturally for 15 minutes; quick release any remaining pressure.

4. Carefully remove the lid, and remove and discard the bay leaf. Taste, and season with salt and pepper, as needed.

INGREDIENT TIP: Both green peas and green split peas are seeds from the same plant, the Pisum sativum. The difference is that the split pea is peeled and dried, which causes it to split.

PER SERVING: Calories: 224; Total fat: 5g; Saturated fat: 2g; Sodium: 743mg; Carbs: 35g; Fiber: 14g; Protein: 13g

PREP TIME:
5 minutes

COOKING
SETTING:
Sauté Low
for 5 minutes;
Manual, High
Pressure for
5 minutes
(4 minutes at
sea level)

RELEASE:
Natural for
15 minutes,
then Quick

TOTAL TIME:
30 minutes

POTATO LEEK SOUP

GLUTEN FREE · NUT FREE

If you're feeling fancy, call this soup by its French name: *potage parmentier!* You can also serve it chilled and call it *vichyssoise.* No matter what you call it, this classic soup is simple yet elegant, quick yet comforting. If you don't have an immersion blender, transfer the soup to your blender in batches, but that can be messy (and dangerous while the soup is hot). I recommend investing in an immersion blender—they're not expensive and so useful for soups, smoothies, and other recipes. **SERVES 4**

3 tablespoons vegan butter

2 large leeks, white and very light green parts only, cleaned well, chopped

2 garlic cloves, minced

4 cups DIY Vegetable Stock (page 154), or store-bought stock

1 pound Yukon Gold potatoes, cubed

1 bay leaf

½ teaspoon salt, plus more as needed

⅔ cup soy milk

⅓ cup extra-virgin olive oil

Freshly ground white pepper

1. On your Instant Pot®, select Sauté Low. When the display reads "Hot," add the butter and leeks. Cook for about 2 to 3 minutes until soft, stirring occasionally. Add the garlic. Cook for 30 to 45 seconds, stirring frequently, until fragrant.

2. Pour in the stock and add the potatoes, bay leaf, and salt. Stir to combine. Lock the lid and turn the steam release handle to Sealing. Using the Manual function, set the cooker to High Pressure for 5 minutes (4 minutes at sea level).

3. When the cook time is complete, let the pressure release naturally for 15 minutes; quick release any remaining pressure.

4. While waiting for the pressure to release, in a blender, combine the soy milk and olive oil. Blend until combined, about 1 minute. This is an easy dairy-free substitute for heavy cream.

5. Carefully remove the lid, remove and discard the bay leaf, and stir in the "cream." Using an immersion blender, purée the soup until smooth. Taste and season with salt and pepper, as desired.

INGREDIENT TIP: If you're not familiar with leeks, the most important thing to know is that you have to rinse them very well—they're grown in sandy soil, which easily collects between the layers.

PER SERVING: Calories: 360; Total fat: 28g; Saturated fat: 6g; Sodium: 632mg; Carbs: 29g; Fiber: 4g; Protein: 4g

PREP TIME:
10 minutes

COOKING
SETTING:
Sauté Low
for 5 minutes;
Manual, High
Pressure for
35 minutes
(30 minutes
at sea level)

RELEASE:
Quick

TOTAL TIME:
50 minutes

COZY WILD RICE SOUP

NUT FREE · SOY FREE

This is the quintessential winter soup, and exactly what you need for a cozy evening spent on your couch binge watching the latest true-crime show. Honestly, sometimes I'll even make it in the summer and just crank up the air-conditioning. Don't tell anyone, okay? I have one other favor to ask: Please use actual wild rice, not just brown rice or even a wild rice blend (see tip). Wild rice has a different flavor and texture that helps make this soup awesome. I promise it is worth it. **SERVES 4 TO 6**

8 tablespoons vegan butter, divided

5 carrots, sliced, with thicker end cut into half-moons

5 celery stalks, sliced

1 small sweet onion, diced

4 garlic cloves, minced

8 ounces baby bella mushrooms, sliced

2 bay leaves

½ teaspoon paprika

½ teaspoon dried thyme

½ teaspoon salt, plus more as needed

4 cups DIY Vegetable Stock (page 154), or store-bought stock

1 cup wild rice

½ cup all-purpose flour

1 cup nondairy milk

Freshly ground black pepper

1. On your Instant Pot®, select Sauté Low. When the display reads "Hot," add 2 tablespoons of butter to melt. Add the carrots, celery, onion, garlic, mushrooms, bay leaves, paprika, thyme, and salt. Cook for 2 to 3 minutes, just until fragrant. Turn off the Instant Pot®.

2. Stir in the stock and wild rice. Lock the lid and turn the steam release handle to Sealing. Using the Manual function, set the cooker to High Pressure for 35 minutes (30 minutes at sea level).

3. When there are just a few minutes of cook time remaining, in a small pan over medium-low heat on your stovetop, melt the remaining 6 tablespoons of butter. Whisk in the flour and cook for 3 to 4 minutes. Whisk in the milk, getting rid of any lumps to finish the roux.

4. When the cook time is complete, quick release the pressure.

5. Carefully remove the lid, and remove and discard the bay leaves. Select Sauté Low again. Stir in the roux and let warm through and thicken. Taste and season with salt and pepper, as needed.

TECHNIQUE TIP: You may be wondering why the roux goes in at the end, when you're used to those steps being first. It's because thickeners such as flour and cornstarch don't work the same in the Instant Pot® as they do on the stovetop. Add them at the end, and they'll work just the way they're meant to!

INGREDIENT TIP: Wild rice (which isn't even actually rice . . . it's grass!) can be found in most health stores and in many grocery stores. A lot of stores don't stock it with the regular rice, but rather with the specialty grains.

PER SERVING: Calories: 480; Total fat: 26g; Saturated fat: 6g; Sodium: 754mg; Carbs: 57g; Fiber: 6g; Protein: 10g

PREP TIME:
5 minutes

COOKING
SETTING:
Sauté Low
for 6 minutes;
Manual, High
Pressure for
30 minutes
(25 minutes
at sea level)

RELEASE:
Quick

TOTAL TIME:
41 minutes

CURRIED SQUASH SOUP

BUDGET FRIENDLY · GLUTEN FREE · SOY FREE

Butternut squash used to be a deal breaker for me during the warmer months. Who wants to run their oven for an hour and heat up the whole kitchen when it's hot outside? So, I'd save the recipe ideas with butternut for fall and winter cooking . . . but not anymore! Now I make rich soups like this one year-round with no fuss. This recipe is particularly good, with its butternut-forward flavor. If you want to add more curry I recommend you wait until the end, after you've blended the soup. **SERVES 4 TO 6**

1 tablespoon olive oil

1 onion, chopped

2 garlic cloves, chopped

1 tablespoon curry powder

1 (2- to 3-pound) butternut squash, peeled and cubed

4 cups DIY Vegetable Stock (page 154), or store-bought stock

1 teaspoon salt

1 (14-ounce) can lite coconut milk

1. On your Instant Pot®, select Sauté Low. When the display reads "Hot," add the oil and heat until it shimmers. Add the onion. Cook for 3 to 4 minutes, stirring frequently. Turn off the Instant Pot® and add the garlic and curry powder. Cook for 1 minute, stirring. It should start smelling delicious right about now!

2. Add the squash, stock, and salt. Lock the lid and turn the steam release handle to Sealing. Using the Manual function, set the cooker to High Pressure for 30 minutes (25 minutes at sea level).

3. When the cook time is complete, quick release the pressure.

4. Carefully remove the lid. Using an immersion blender, blend the soup until completely smooth. Stir in the coconut milk, saving a little bit for topping when served.

PER SERVING: Calories: 267; Total fat: 11g; Saturated fat: 7g; Sodium: 843mg; Carbs: 50g; Fiber: 8g; Protein: 5g

SMOKY WHITE BEAN SOUP

BUDGET FRIENDLY · GLUTEN FREE · SOY FREE

I made this thick and hearty soup on the stovetop for years before I got my first Instant Pot®, and I think it's the perfect example of why electric pressure cookers are so brilliant. Combine your ingredients, turn it on, and then go do the things you'd rather be doing. Be sure to use smoked paprika rather than the sweet variety. The depth of flavor that spice gives is amazing! **SERVES 4 TO 6**

PREP TIME:
3 minutes

COOKING SETTING:
Manual, High Pressure for 32 minutes (27 minutes at sea level)

RELEASE:
Natural for 10 minutes, then Quick

TOTAL TIME:
45 minutes

1 cup dried great northern white beans, rinsed

1 small to medium tomato, diced

¼ cup raw millet

1 cube vegetable or "not chicken" bouillon

1 to 1½ teaspoons smoked paprika, plus more as needed

1 teaspoon salt, plus more as needed

3½ to 4 cups water, plus more as needed

1 (14-ounce) can lite coconut milk

1 cup frozen sweet corn

1. In your Instant Pot®, stir together the beans, tomato, millet, bouillon cube, paprika, salt, water, and coconut milk. Lock the lid and turn the steam release handle to Sealing. Using the Manual function, set the cooker to High Pressure for 32 minutes (27 minutes at sea level).

2. When the cook time is complete, turn off the Instant Pot® (don't let it go into Keep Warm mode) and let the pressure release naturally for 10 minutes; quick release any remaining pressure.

3. Carefully remove the lid and stir in the corn. Taste and adjust the seasonings, as needed.

MAKE-AHEAD TIP: This soup thickens as it cools, so if you're saving some for leftovers, have additional water or nondairy milk on hand when you're ready to reheat.

PER SERVING: Calories: 183; Total fat: 7g; Saturated fat: 6g; Sodium: 864mg; Carbs: 27g; Fiber: 4g; Protein: 6g

PREP TIME:
5 minutes

COOKING SETTING:
Sauté Low for 6 minutes; Manual, High Pressure for 4 minutes (3 minutes at sea level)

RELEASE:
Quick

TOTAL TIME:
15 minutes

MINESTRONE SOUP

BUDGET FRIENDLY • NUT FREE • SOY FREE

Minestrone soup is something I grew up eating, but never knew much about—and it has a really interesting backstory. The word *minestrone* literally translates to "big soup," indicating its origin is likely based on collecting the small amounts of leftover ingredients from previous meals and combining them into one *big soup* so as not to waste anything. As someone who is very frugal, this makes sense to me. Minestrone might actually be my spirit soup! **SERVES 4 TO 6**

2 tablespoons olive oil

2 celery stalks, sliced

1 sweet onion, diced

1 large carrot, sliced, with thicker end cut into half-moons

2 garlic cloves, minced

1 teaspoon dried oregano

1 teaspoon dried basil

½ to 1 teaspoon salt, plus more as needed

1 bay leaf

1 zucchini, roughly diced

1 (28-ounce) can diced tomatoes

1 (16-ounce) can kidney beans, drained and rinsed

1 cup small dried pasta

6 cups DIY Vegetable Stock (page 154), or store-bought stock

2 to 3 cups fresh baby spinach

Freshly ground black pepper

1. On your Instant Pot®, select Sauté Low. When the display reads "Hot," add the oil, celery, onion, and carrot. Cook for 2 to 3 minutes, stirring frequently. Add the garlic and cook for another minute or so, stirring frequently. Turn off the Instant Pot® and add the oregano, basil, salt, and bay leaf. Stir and let sit for 30 seconds to 1 minute.

2. Add the zucchini, tomatoes, kidney beans, pasta, and stock. Lock the lid and turn the steam release handle to Sealing. Using the Manual function, set the cooker to High Pressure for 4 minutes (3 minutes at sea level).

3. When the cook time is complete, quick release the pressure.

4. Carefully remove the lid, and remove and discard the bay leaf. Stir in the spinach and let it get all nice and wilty. Taste and season with more salt, as needed, and pepper. Serve hot.

PER SERVING: Calories: 332; Total fat: 12g; Saturated fat: 4g; Sodium: 654mg; Carbs: 54g; Fiber: 12g; Protein: 13g

LASAGNA SOUP

NUT FREE • SOY FREE

Lasagna. Soup. Both are wonderful comfort foods. My preferred method of eating this involves sweatpants and my couch, but if you're serving it to guests, tell them how the word *lasagna* is derived from the Greek word for pasta, *laganon*, and have a spirited debate on whether this dish should really be considered Italian. **SERVES 4 TO 6**

PREP TIME:
5 minutes

COOKING SETTING:
Sauté Low for 5 minutes; Manual, High Pressure for 4 minutes (3 minutes at sea level)

RELEASE:
Natural for 10 minutes, then Quick

TOTAL TIME:
24 minutes

1 to 2 tablespoons olive oil

1 medium onion, diced

1 garlic clove, diced

2 teaspoons dried oregano

1 teaspoon dried rosemary

½ to ¾ teaspoon red pepper flakes

½ teaspoon salt

2 tomatoes, chopped

1 cube vegetable or "not chicken" bouillon

1 bay leaf

10 lasagna noodles, broken into bite-size pieces

½ to ⅔ cup red sauce (there are two delicious options in chapter 9, see pages 155 and 156!)

6 cups water

Salt

Freshly ground black pepper

Fresh basil, for garnishing (optional)

Shredded vegan mozzarella cheese, for garnishing (optional)

1. On your Instant Pot®, select Sauté Low. When the display reads "Hot," add the oil and heat until it shimmers. Add the onion. Sauté for 2 to 3 minutes until softened. Add the garlic and immediately turn off the pressure cooker. Keep stirring as the garlic cooks (don't let it burn).

2. Add the oregano, rosemary, red pepper flakes, salt, tomatoes, bouillon cube, bay leaf, noodles, red sauce, and water. Stir well to combine. You want the noodles to be submerged. Lock the lid and turn the steam release handle to Sealing. Using the Manual function, set the cooker to High Pressure for 4 minutes (3 minutes at sea level).

3. When the cook time is complete, turn off the Instant Pot® and let the pressure release naturally for 10 minutes; quick release any remaining pressure. Carefully remove the lid, and remove and discard the bay leaf. Taste and season with salt and pepper, as desired, and serve with your favorite toppings!

PER SERVING: Calories: 311; Total fat: 9g; Saturated fat: 1g; Sodium: 754mg; Carbs: 50g; Fiber: 3g; Protein: 10g

PREP TIME:
4 minutes

**COOKING
SETTING:**
Sauté Low
for 5 minutes;
Manual, High
Pressure for
6 minutes
(5 minutes at
sea level)

RELEASE:
Quick

TOTAL TIME:
15 minutes

MOM'S CORN CHOWDER

BUDGET FRIENDLY · SOY FREE

This corn chowder is my childhood in a bowl. It's a version of the chowder my mom always made, which was hearty and delicious and something I requested often. It was also very much not vegan, which led to my quest to create the most compassionate and tasty version possible. This is my latest iteration, which in addition to being highly crave-able is also very quick to make, thanks to the magic of pressure cooking. Plus it is mom approved, so you know it stands up well to the original! **SERVES 4 TO 6**

1 tablespoon olive oil

1 small sweet onion, diced

3 celery stalks, sliced

2 garlic cloves, minced

1 teaspoon dried thyme

½ teaspoon ground coriander

½ to 1 teaspoon salt

¼ teaspoon freshly ground black pepper

3 medium to large russet potatoes, peeled and cut into large dice

3½ cups DIY Vegetable Stock (page 154), or store-bought stock

6 tablespoons vegan butter

½ cup all-purpose flour

1 cup nondairy milk

12 ounces frozen sweet corn

1 carrot, grated

Sliced scallion, green and light green parts, for garnishing (optional)

1. On your Instant Pot®, select Sauté Low. When the display reads "Hot," add the oil and heat until it shimmers. Add the onion. Cook for 2 to 3 minutes, stirring frequently. Turn off the Instant Pot® and add the celery, garlic, thyme, coriander, salt, and pepper. Cook for another minute or so (the inner pot is still hot).

2. Stir in the potatoes and stock. Lock the lid and turn the steam release handle to Sealing. Using the Manual function, set the cooker to High Pressure for 6 minutes (5 minutes at sea level).

3. While the chowder cooks, in a small pan over medium-low heat on the stovetop, melt the butter. Whisk in the flour and cook for 3 to 4 minutes. Whisk in the milk, getting rid of any lumps to finish the roux.

4. When the cook time is complete, quick release the pressure.

5. Carefully remove the lid and select Sauté Low again. Add the corn and carrot. Stir in the roux and let warm through and thicken. Taste and season with salt and pepper, as desired. Garnish with scallion (if using) before serving.

> **SERVING TIP:** Make this chowder a little more fun by serving it in a bread bowl. Sourdough is my favorite, but any type of bread will do—just don't forget the vegan butter!

PER SERVING: Calories: 413; Total fat: 24g; Saturated fat: 5g; Sodium: 643mg; Carbs: 49g; Fiber: 6g; Protein: 6g

PREP TIME:
3 minutes

COOKING SETTING:
Manual, High Pressure for 2 minutes

RELEASE:
Natural for 5 minutes, then Quick

TOTAL TIME:
10 minutes

CHIPOTLE SWEET POTATO CHOWDER

GLUTEN FREE · SOY FREE

I first made this chowder years ago, on the stovetop, and fell in love. It's a dish I've returned to over and over again, which is high praise coming from a food blogger who is always coming up with new recipes! I especially like how easy it is to adjust the heat levels to match my audience. When I'm making it for my mom, I use only two chipotle peppers. Making it for friends from New Mexico? Four peppers, plus a few tablespoons of adobo sauce (at least!). **SERVES 4 TO 6**

1¼ cups DIY Vegetable Stock (page 154), or store-bought stock

1 (14-ounce) can lite coconut milk

2 large sweet potatoes, peeled and diced large

2 to 4 canned chipotle peppers in adobo sauce, diced

1 red bell pepper, diced

1 small onion, diced

1 teaspoon ground cumin

½ to 1 teaspoon salt

1½ cups frozen sweet corn

Adobo sauce from the canned peppers, to taste

1. In a medium bowl, whisk the stock and coconut milk, ensuring there are no solid bits of coconut milk left. Pour into the Instant Pot® and add the sweet potatoes, chipotles, bell pepper, onion, cumin, and salt. Lock the lid and turn the steam release handle to Sealing. Using the Manual function, set the cooker to High pressure for 2 minutes.

2. When the cook time is complete, let the pressure release naturally for 5 minutes; quick release any remaining pressure.

3. Carefully remove the lid and add the frozen corn and adobo sauce, if you want more heat. Let sit for 1 to 2 minutes while the corn warms.

MAKE-AHEAD TIP: The flavors just get better after this chowder sits overnight in the fridge, so make extra to take for lunches!

PER SERVING: Calories: 216; Total fat: 10g; Saturated fat: 7g; Sodium: 987mg; Carbs: 35g; Fiber: 6g; Protein: 5g

COCONUT SWEET POTATO STEW

GLUTEN FREE · SOY FREE

This savory stew is so versatile (increase the chili powder for more heat, or add a cup of cooked quinoa for heartiness), but to me, it's perfect the way it is. One tip to keep in mind: When using canned coconut milk in the Instant Pot®, shake it very well to ensure the parts are combined. Any bits of the thicker coconut milk may separate and become grainy during cooking. **SERVES 4 TO 6**

PREP TIME:
5 minutes

COOKING SETTING:
Sauté Low for 5 minutes; Manual, High Pressure for 5 minutes (4 minutes at sea level)

RELEASE:
Natural for 10 minutes, then Quick

TOTAL TIME:
25 minutes

2 tablespoons avocado or olive oil

½ sweet onion, diced

2 sweet potatoes, peeled and cubed

2 garlic cloves, minced

1 to 1½ teaspoons salt

1 teaspoon ground turmeric

1 teaspoon paprika

½ teaspoon ground cumin

½ teaspoon dried oregano

1 or 2 dashes chili powder

2 Roma tomatoes, chopped

1 (14-ounce) can lite coconut milk, shaken well

1¼ cups water, plus more as needed

1 to 2 cups chopped kale

1. On your Instant Pot®, select Sauté Low. When the display reads "Hot," add the oil and heat until it shimmers. Add the onion. Cook for 2 to 3 minutes, stirring frequently. If they start to burn, hit the Cancel button and let the pot cool down a little before turning it back on.

2. Stir in the sweet potatoes, garlic, salt, turmeric, paprika, cumin, oregano, and chili powder. Stir, stir, stir and cook for 1 minute or so. Add the tomatoes, coconut milk, and water and give it one last good stir. Lock the lid and turn the steam release handle to Sealing. Using the Manual function, set the cooker to High Pressure for 5 minutes (4 minutes at sea level).

3. When the cook time is complete, turn off the Instant Pot®. Let the pressure release naturally for 10 minutes; quick release any remaining pressure.

4. Carefully remove the lid and stir in the kale, which will wilt quickly. Add more water if you want a thinner consistency.

PER SERVING: Calories: 224; Total fat: 13g; Saturated fat: 7g; Sodium: 431mg; Carbs: 26g; Fiber: 4g; Protein: 5g

PREP TIME:
5 minutes

COOKING
SETTING:
Sauté Low
for 4 minutes;
Manual, High
Pressure for
8 minutes
(7 minutes at
sea level)

RELEASE:
Natural for
10 minutes,
then Quick

TOTAL TIME:
27 minutes

CIAMBOTTA

BUDGET FRIENDLY • GLUTEN FREE • NUT FREE • SOY FREE

This Italian vegetable stew has always intrigued me. Growing up in the States, stew is generally considered a winter dish. Italians, however, make it with summer garden plants such as eggplant, tomatoes, and basil. This is a delicious way to eat your veggies, and you can make it without ever heating up your kitchen. **SERVES 4 TO 6**

1 to 2 tablespoons olive oil

2 leeks, white and very light green parts only, cleaned well, halved lengthwise, cut into half-moons

1 sweet onion, cut into large dice

1 carrot, halved lengthwise, cut into half-moons

1 celery stalk, sliced

1 cup sliced white mushrooms

1 small eggplant, cut into large dice

3 garlic cloves, minced

3 Yukon Gold potatoes, chopped into large bite-size pieces

3 Roma tomatoes, cut into large dice

4 cups DIY Vegetable Stock (page 154), or store-bought stock

1 teaspoon dried oregano

½ teaspoon salt, plus more as needed

2 cups torn kale leaves

Freshly ground black pepper

Fresh basil, for garnishing

1. On your Instant Pot®, select Sauté Low. When the display reads "Hot," add the oil and heat until it shimmers. Add the leeks, onion, carrot, celery, mushrooms, and eggplant. Cook for about 2 minutes, stirring occasionally. Add the garlic. Cook for 30 seconds more. Turn off the Instant Pot® and add the potatoes, tomatoes, stock, oregano, and salt. Lock the lid and turn the steam release handle to Sealing. Using the Manual function, set the cooker to High Pressure for 8 minutes (7 minutes at sea level).

2. When the cook time is complete, let the pressure release naturally for 10 minutes; quick release any remaining pressure.

3. Carefully remove the lid and stir in the kale. Taste and season with more salt, as needed, and pepper. If there's too much liquid, select Sauté Low again and cook for a few minutes to evaporate. Serve garnished with basil.

PER SERVING: Calories: 285; Total fat: 8g; Saturated fat: 1g; Sodium: 347mg; Carbs: 51g; Fiber: 12g; Protein: 8g

WHITE BEAN & SWISS CHARD STEW

BUDGET FRIENDLY · GLUTEN FREE · NUT FREE · SOY FREE

Sometimes in pressure cooking, the cook times of the beans and the vegetables just don't match up—hence this recipe's use of precooked beans to avoid soggy veggies. This is a great opportunity to utilize meal prep with an extra batch of beans, as with the Quick Double Bean Chili (page 78). You can also use canned beans if you prefer. **SERVES 4 TO 6**

PREP TIME:
6 minutes

COOKING SETTING:
Sauté Low for 5 minutes; Manual, High Pressure for 4 minutes (3 minutes at sea level)

RELEASE:
Quick

TOTAL TIME:
15 minutes

1 tablespoon olive oil

2 carrots, sliced, with thicker end cut into half-moons

1 celery stalk, sliced

½ onion, cut into large dice

2 or 3 garlic cloves, minced

3 tomatoes, chopped

¼ to ½ teaspoon red pepper flakes

½ teaspoon dried rosemary

½ teaspoon dried oregano

¼ teaspoon dried basil

½ teaspoon salt, plus more as needed

Pinch freshly ground black pepper, plus more as needed

2 cups cooked great northern beans

1 small bunch Swiss chard leaves, chopped

Nutritional yeast, for sprinkling (optional)

1. On your Instant Pot®, select Sauté Low. When the display reads "Hot," add the oil and heat until it shimmers. Add the carrots, celery, and onion. Cook for 2 to 3 minutes, stirring occasionally. Add the garlic and cook for 30 seconds more. Turn off the Instant Pot®.

2. Stir in the tomatoes, red pepper flakes, rosemary, oregano, basil, salt, pepper, and beans. Lock the lid and turn the steam release handle to Sealing. Using the Manual function, set the cooker to High Pressure for 4 minutes (3 minutes at sea level).

3. When the cook time is complete, quick release the pressure.

4. Carefully remove the lid and stir in the Swiss chard. Let wilt for 2 to 3 minutes. Taste and season with salt and pepper, as needed, and sprinkle the nutritional yeast over individual servings (if using).

PER SERVING: Calories: 174; Total fat: 4g; Saturated fat: 1g; Sodium: 324mg; Carbs: 29g; Fiber: 9g; Protein: 9g

PREP TIME:
7 minutes

COOKING
SETTING:
Sauté Low
for 5 minutes;
Manual, High
Pressure for
3 minutes

RELEASE:
Quick

TOTAL TIME:
15 minutes

AFRICAN PEANUT STEW

BUDGET FRIENDLY · GLUTEN FREE · SOY FREE

Oh, the heady flavor of this stew! This dish brings so many different notes together—from the earthy roasted walnut oil to the sweet-hot zing of the fresh ginger to the rich saltiness of the peanuts and peanut butter. This is also a great excuse to use collard greens, a veggie I don't use often enough. The thick leaves really stand up to the flavorful stew. If you don't have access to collards, kale works well. **SERVES 4 TO 6**

1 tablespoon roasted walnut oil

1 small onion, cut into large dice

1 red bell pepper, cut into large dice

1 jalapeño pepper, diced

3 garlic cloves, minced

3 tomatoes, cut into large dice

1 sweet potato, cut into large dice

2 tablespoons minced peeled fresh ginger

1½ teaspoons ground cumin

½ teaspoon chili powder

½ teaspoon salt, plus more as needed

½ cup creamy all-natural peanut butter (not sweetened)

2 cups DIY Vegetable Stock (page 154), or store-bought stock, divided

1 small bunch collard green leaves, chopped

Freshly ground black pepper

½ cup chopped roasted peanuts

1. On your Instant Pot®, select Sauté Low. When the display reads "Hot," add the oil and heat until it shimmers. Add the onion, bell pepper, and jalapeño. Cook for 2 to 3 minutes, stirring frequently. Turn off the Instant Pot® and add the garlic. Cook for 30 seconds, stirring.

2. Stir in the tomatoes, sweet potato, ginger, cumin, chili powder, and salt. Let rest for a few minutes.

3. While the stew rests, in a large measuring cup, whisk the peanut butter and 1 cup of stock until smooth. Pour this into the Instant Pot®. Use the remaining 1 cup of stock to rinse out the measuring cup, making sure you get as much of the peanut butter as possible. Add this to the pot. Lock the lid and turn the steam release handle to Sealing. Using the Manual function, set the cooker to High Pressure for 3 minutes.

4. When the cook time is complete, quick release the pressure.

5. Carefully remove the lid and stir in the collard greens, which will wilt in 1 to 2 minutes. Taste and season with salt and pepper, as needed, and serve topped with chopped peanuts.

MAKE-AHEAD TIP: This stew is great to make on a Sunday and enjoy the leftovers—I love reheating it for lunch throughout the week.

PER SERVING: Calories: 602; Total fat: 46g; Saturated fat: 5g; Sodium: 456mg; Carbs: 33g; Fiber: 14g; Protein: 22g

BUTTERNUT QUINOA CHILI

BUDGET FRIENDLY · GLUTEN FREE · NUT FREE · SOY FREE

When I first went vegetarian, and then vegan, chili was one of the foods I thought I was just going to have to learn to live without. I didn't cook much back then, and the idea of just combining a few cans of beans and calling it chili made me sad. It wasn't until I became more comfortable with vegan cooking that I realized there is a whole universe of flavor out there, just waiting to be made into chili! So I started to experiment, and this butternut and quinoa combo remains one of my favorites. **SERVES 4 TO 6**

PREP TIME:
5 minutes

COOKING SETTING:
Sauté Low for 5 minutes; Manual, High Pressure for 8 minutes (7 minutes at sea level)

RELEASE:
Natural for 10 minutes, then Quick

TOTAL TIME:
28 minutes

1 to 2 tablespoons olive oil

2 carrots, sliced

1 sweet onion, cut into large dice

1 red bell pepper, cut into large dice

1 jalapeño pepper, diced

2 garlic cloves, minced

1 butternut squash, peeled and cut into bite-size cubes

1 (14-ounce) can diced tomatoes with juice

1 cup uncooked quinoa, rinsed

2½ cups DIY Vegetable Stock (page 154), or store-bought stock

1 bay leaf

1 teaspoon ground cumin

½ to 1 teaspoon salt, plus more as needed

½ teaspoon sweet paprika

½ teaspoon chili powder, or more to taste

½ teaspoon freshly ground black pepper, plus more as needed

1 tablespoon freshly squeezed lemon juice

1. On your Instant Pot®, select Sauté Low. When the display reads "Hot," add the oil and heat until it shimmers. Add the carrots, onion, bell pepper, and jalapeño. Cook for 2 to 3 minutes, stirring. Turn off the Instant Pot® and add the garlic, stirring again so it doesn't burn.

2. Add the squash, tomatoes, quinoa, stock, bay leaf, cumin, salt, paprika, chili powder, and pepper. Lock the lid and turn the steam release handle to Sealing. Using the Manual function, set the cooker to High Pressure for 8 minutes (7 minutes at sea level).

3. When the cook time is complete, turn the Instant Pot® off and let the pressure release naturally for 10 minutes; quick release any remaining pressure.

4. Carefully remove the lid. Remove and discard the bay leaf, and stir in the lemon juice. Taste and season with salt and pepper, as needed. If there's too much liquid, select Sauté Low again and cook for 1 to 2 minutes, stirring frequently.

MAKE-AHEAD TIP: This chili is excellent to make ahead and freeze. The flavors just get better and better!

PER SERVING: Calories: 325; Total fat: 7g; Saturated fat: 1g; Sodium: 333mg; Carbs: 61g; Fiber: 10g; Protein: 10g

PREP TIME:
10 minutes

COOKING SETTING:
Sauté Low for 8 minutes; Manual, High Pressure for 5 minutes (4 minutes at sea level)

RELEASE:
Quick

TOTAL TIME:
23 minutes

QUICK DOUBLE BEAN CHILI

BUDGET FRIENDLY • GLUTEN FREE • NUT FREE • SOY FREE

Canned beans make this comforting chili (perfect after a long, cold day) super easy to make. You could also go the meal prep route and cook up a couple batches of beans to have ready to use throughout the week. Personally, I'm a big believer in meal prepping on Sunday afternoons, as I find it effective and frugal. Either way, I hope you enjoy this chili! **SERVES 4 TO 6**

¾ cup water, divided, plus more as needed

½ sweet onion, chopped

1 jalapeño pepper, seeded and diced

3 garlic cloves, diced

1 bell pepper, any color, chopped

1 sweet potato, peeled and chopped

1 teaspoon salt, plus more as needed

2 teaspoons ground cumin

1 teaspoon smoked paprika

1½ teaspoons dried oregano

1 teaspoon red pepper flakes

½ to 1 teaspoon chili powder, plus more as needed

1 (15-ounce) can black beans, drained and rinsed

1 (15-ounce) can kidney beans, drained and rinsed

1 (28-ounce) can fire-roasted diced tomatoes, with liquid

¼ cup barbecue sauce

Cashew Sour Cream (page 160), for topping (optional)

Chopped avocado, for topping (optional)

Chopped onion, for topping (optional)

Fresh basil, for topping (optional)

Fresh cilantro, for topping (optional)

Crumbled tortilla chips, for topping (optional)

1. On your Instant Pot®, select Sauté Low. When the display reads "Hot," add ¼ cup of water, the onion, jalapeño, and garlic. Cook for 2 to 3 minutes, stirring frequently.

2. Add the bell pepper and sweet potato. Cook for 2 to 3 minutes more, stirring occasionally and adding water if necessary (you really only need a tiny bit of water in there).

3. Add the salt, cumin, paprika, oregano, red pepper flakes, chili powder, black beans, kidney beans, tomatoes, and remaining ½ cup of water. Stir well so the spices are mixed in. Lock the lid and turn the steam release handle to Sealing. Using the Manual function, set the cooker to High Pressure for 5 minutes (4 minutes at sea level).

4. When the cook time is complete, quick release the pressure.

5. Carefully remove the lid and stir in the barbecue sauce. Taste and add salt or more chili powder, as needed, as well as your favorite toppings!

INGREDIENT TIP: I go for a sweet onion and a sweet barbecue sauce because I really enjoy the hint of sweetness they bring to this spicy chili!

PER SERVING: Calories: 335; Total fat: 2g; Saturated fat: 0g; Sodium: 1115mg; Carbs: 66g; Fiber: 19g; Protein: 18g

PREP TIME:
10 minutes

COOKING
SETTING:
Sauté Low for
11 minutes;
Manual, High
Pressure for
5 minutes
(4 minutes at
sea level)

RELEASE:
Natural for
10 minutes,
then Quick

TOTAL TIME:
36 minutes

TACO CHILI

BUDGET FRIENDLY · NUT FREE

Can't decide between tacos or chili for dinner? Have both! I really think you'll love the way this chili tastes—and the way it makes your kitchen smell! When the smoked paprika heats up and becomes fragrant, your tummy is guaranteed to start growling. And don't skimp on the toppings, they're what really create the feeling of tacos. My ideal way to eat this chili is with my bowl piled high with avocado and scallions, and a second bowl full of tortilla chips for dipping. Who needs a spoon? **SERVES 6 TO 8**

2 tablespoons olive oil

1 (8-ounce) package unflavored tempeh, cut into large dice

1 teaspoon smoked paprika

1 small onion, diced

1 green bell pepper, diced

1 jalapeño pepper, diced

1 (15-ounce) can diced tomatoes with green chilies, drained

1 (15-ounce) can black beans, rinsed and drained

1 (16-ounce) can chili beans, undrained

1 teaspoon ground cumin

1 teaspoon salt

½ teaspoon garlic powder

½ teaspoon chili powder, plus more as needed

Chopped scallion, green and light green parts, for garnishing

Chopped avocado or Cashew Sour Cream (page 160), for garnishing

Shredded vegan cheese, for sprinkling

Tortilla chips, for serving

1. On your Instant Pot®, select Sauté Low. When the display reads "Hot," add the oil and heat until it shimmers. Add the tempeh and paprika. Cook for 6 to 7 minutes, stirring frequently. The tempeh will break down a bit, and that's fine.

2. Add the onion, bell pepper, and jalapeño. Sauté for 2 to 3 minutes more, or until soft. Add 1 to 2 tablespoons of water, if things are sticking. Turn off the Instant Pot®.

3. Stir in the tomatoes and green chilies, black beans, chili beans, cumin, salt, garlic powder, and chili powder to taste. Lock the lid and turn the steam release handle to Sealing. Using the Manual function set the cooker to High Pressure for 5 minutes (4 minutes at sea level).

4. When the cook time is complete, let the pressure release naturally for 10 minutes; quick release any remaining pressure. Carefully remove the lid. If the chili is too thin, select Sauté Low again and cook until the desired consistency is reached. Serve topped as you like.

LEFTOVER TIP: Try serving the rest of this chili over baked sweet potatoes for a fun twist on leftover night.

PER SERVING: Calories: 334; Total fat: 16g; Saturated fat: 3g; Sodium: 877mg; Carbs: 35g; Fiber: 10g; Protein: 19g

Creamy
Veggie Risotto

6

BEANS, LEGUMES &
GRAINS

PREP TIME:
15 minutes

COOKING SETTING:
Sauté Low for 4 minutes; Manual, High Pressure for 35 minutes (30 minutes at sea level); Sauté Medium for 5 to 10 minutes

RELEASE:
Natural for 20 minutes

TOTAL TIME:
1 hour 24 minutes

GREEN CHILE BAKED BEANS

NUT FREE • SOY FREE

The next time you're faced with being the only vegan at a barbecue, bring these next-level baked beans and win some people over! These are a million times better than canned, especially with the added smoky flavor of roasted green chile. You could also try adding a splash of bourbon to the molasses mix . . . I won't tell! **SERVES 4 TO 6**

¼ cup blackstrap molasses

¼ cup maple syrup

¼ cup packed light brown sugar

2 tablespoons ketchup

1 tablespoon vegan Worcestershire sauce

1 tablespoon olive oil

1 small sweet onion, cut into large dice

3 or 4 garlic cloves, minced

1 teaspoon salt

1 pound dried navy beans, soaked in water overnight, rinsed, and drained

1½ cups diced roasted green chiles (freshly roasted Hatch or poblanos, or from a can)

1 teaspoon apple cider vinegar

1. In a small bowl, whisk the molasses, maple syrup, brown sugar, ketchup, and Worcestershire sauce. Set aside.

2. On your Instant Pot®, select Sauté Low. When the display reads "Hot," add the oil and heat until it shimmers. Add the onion and garlic. Turn off the Instant Pot® and sauté the veggies for 1 to 2 minutes, stirring frequently. Add the salt, beans, and molasses mix, stirring well. Lock the lid and turn the steam release handle to Sealing. Using the Manual function, set the cooker to High Pressure for 35 minutes (30 minutes at sea level).

3. When the cook time is complete, let the pressure release naturally for 20 minutes, or until the pin drops.

4. Carefully remove the lid and stir. Select Sauté Medium. Stir in the green chiles and simmer the beans for 5 to 10 minutes, or until the sauce thickens.

5. Stir in the vinegar and serve.

PER SERVING: Calories: 435; Total fat: 4g; Saturated fat: 1g; Sodium: 947mg; Carbs: 89g; Fiber: 19g; Protein: 21g

MEXICAN BLACK BEANS

BUDGET FRIENDLY · GLUTEN FREE · NUT FREE · SOY FREE

People from New Mexico will tell you Hatch green chiles are best. People from Colorado might argue for Pueblo chiles. Poblano, Anaheim, serrano . . . there's no wrong choice—they all work amazingly well with black beans! **SERVES 6 TO 8**

PREP TIME:
5 minutes

COOKING SETTING:
Sauté Low for 3 minutes; Manual, High Pressure 35 minutes (30 minutes at sea level)

RELEASE:
Natural for 20 minutes

TOTAL TIME:
1 hour 3 minutes

1 to 2 tablespoons olive oil

1 small onion, diced

3 or 4 garlic cloves, diced

1 tablespoon ground cumin

1 teaspoon dried oregano

1 teaspoon chili powder

1 cup diced roasted green chiles (freshly roasted Hatch chiles or from a can)

3 cups DIY Vegetable Stock (page 154), or store-bought stock

2 cups dried black beans, rinsed but not soaked

½ to 1 teaspoon salt, plus more as needed

2 tablespoons freshly squeezed lime juice

¼ cup fresh cilantro leaves, chopped

1. On your Instant Pot®, select Sauté Low. When the display reads "Hot," add the oil and onion. Sauté for 1 to 2 minutes, turning off the Instant Pot® after about 1 minute. Add the garlic. Sauté for 30 seconds. Stir in the cumin, oregano, and chili powder, and cook for another 30 seconds or so until the spices "bloom" (become very fragrant). Add the green chiles, stock, and black beans, stirring well. Lock the lid and turn the steam release handle to Sealing. Using the Manual function, set the cooker to High Pressure for 35 minutes (30 minutes at sea level).

2. When the cook time is complete, let the pressure release naturally for 20 minutes, or until the pin drops.

3. Carefully remove the lid and stir. Add the salt, lime juice, and cilantro. Stir again and serve.

INGREDIENT TIP: Freshly roasted green chiles are preferable, but most grocery stores also carry canned Hatch green chiles.

PER SERVING: Calories: 287; Total fat: 5g; Saturated fat: 2g; Sodium: 439mg; Carbs: 50g; Fiber: 11g; Protein: 17g

PREP TIME:
2 minutes

COOKING
SETTING:
Manual, High
Pressure for
38 minutes
(32 minutes
at sea level)

RELEASE:
Natural
for 15 to
20 minutes

TOTAL TIME:
1 hour

REFRIED PINTO BEANS

BUDGET FRIENDLY • GLUTEN FREE • NUT FREE • SOY FREE

Refried beans were one of the best parts of eating at Mexican restaurants, so you can imagine my feelings when I went vegetarian, and then vegan, and could no longer enjoy them (most restaurant versions aren't veggie friendly). I like to make this version in my Instant Pot® while the rest of the meal (usually enchiladas) bakes away. Definitely consider adding more jalapeño or chili powder if you're a heat lover! **SERVES 6 TO 8**

1 tablespoon olive oil

1 onion, quartered

3 garlic cloves, peeled

1 pound dried pinto beans, rinsed

2 quarts DIY Vegetable Stock (page 154), or store-bought stock

1 teaspoon ground cumin

1 teaspoon dried Mexican oregano

½ teaspoon chili powder

¼ teaspoon freshly ground black pepper

1 tablespoon freshly squeezed lime juice

1 tablespoon salt, plus more as needed

1. In your Instant Pot®, combine the oil, onion, garlic, beans, stock, cumin, oregano, chili powder, and pepper. Lock the lid and turn the steam release handle to Sealing. Using the Manual function, set the cooker to High Pressure for 38 minutes (32 minutes at sea level).

2. When the cook time is complete, let the pressure release naturally for about 20 minutes, or until the pin drops.

3. Carefully remove the lid and use a ladle to remove most of the remaining liquid, saving it. Using an immersion blender, blend the beans until smooth, adding the cooking water back in as needed.

4. Stir in the lime juice and salt.

TECHNIQUE TIP: Yes, you're cooking these beans longer than normal. That's because you want them extra soft so they blend nice and smooth.

PER SERVING: Calories: 310; Total fat: 6g; Saturated fat: 3g; Sodium: 720mg; Carbs: 53g; Fiber: 12g; Protein: 17g

RED BEANS & RICE

GLUTEN FREE • NUT FREE • SOY FREE

I've been to New Orleans twice—and loved every minute of it. From the grand old homes of the Garden District to the artsy vibe of Jackson Square, there is so much to see and do. And eat! Red beans and rice have traditionally been enjoyed there on Mondays, to balance out the decadence of the preceding weekend. The Instant Pot® makes this meal even easier for a busy Monday dinner by speeding up the bean component. Prepare your favorite white rice on the stovetop and dinner is served! **SERVES 4 TO 6**

PREP TIME:
5 minutes

COOKING SETTING:
Sauté Low for 6 minutes; Manual, High Pressure for 40 minutes (34 minutes at sea level)

RELEASE:
Natural for 25 minutes

TOTAL TIME:
1 hour 16 minutes

1 tablespoon olive oil

1 red onion, diced

1 bell pepper, any color, diced

2 celery stalks, sliced

4 or 5 garlic cloves, minced

2 bay leaves

2 teaspoons Cajun seasoning

½ teaspoon dried oregano

½ teaspoon dried parsley

2 cups dried red beans

4 cups DIY Vegetable Stock (page 154), or store-bought stock

Salt

Freshly ground black pepper

4 to 5 cups cooked white rice

Chopped fresh parsley, for garnishing

Hot sauce, for serving

1. On your Instant Pot®, select Sauté Low. When the display reads "Hot," add the oil and heat until it shimmers. Add the red onion, bell pepper, and celery. Cook for 3 to 4 minutes, stirring frequently. Turn off the Instant Pot® and add the garlic, bay leaves, Cajun seasoning, oregano, and dried parsley. Continue to cook for 1 minute more, stirring.

2. Stir in the beans and stock. Lock the lid and turn the steam release handle to Sealing. Using the Manual function, set the cooker to High Pressure for 40 minutes (34 minutes at sea level).

3. When the cook time is complete, let the pressure release naturally for about 25 minutes, or until the pin drops.

4. Carefully remove the lid, and remove and discard the bay leaves. Taste and season with salt and pepper, as needed. Serve with rice and top with parsley and hot sauce.

PER SERVING: Calories: 609; Total fat: 5g; Saturated fat: 1g; Sodium: 312mg; Carbs: 116g; Fiber: 15g; Protein: 26g

PREP TIME:
5 minutes

COOKING
SETTING:
Manual, High
Pressure for
45 minutes
(38 minutes
at sea level)

RELEASE:
Natural for
20 minutes,
then Quick

TOTAL TIME:
1 hour
10 minutes

CHICKPEA BASIL SALAD

BUDGET FRIENDLY • GLUTEN FREE • NUT FREE • SOY FREE

Once in a while you stumble upon a recipe that seems too good to be true, until you taste it. This is that recipe! The ingredients seem so simple, but the final product truly is delicious. I love that you can throw the chickpeas into the Instant Pot® and go do something else, then come back and whip up the rest. In warmer months, this is one of my go-to dinners because it is satisfying without being heavy. You can also serve it as a side dish in smaller portions. **SERVES 2 TO 4**

1 cup dried chickpeas, rinsed

1 quart water, or enough to cover the chickpeas by 3 to 4 inches

1 cup fresh basil leaves, chopped or sliced

1½ cups grape tomatoes, halved

2 to 3 tablespoons balsamic vinegar

½ teaspoon garlic powder

½ teaspoon salt, plus more as needed

1. In your Instant Pot®, combine the chickpeas and water. Lock the lid and turn the steam release handle to Sealing. Using the Manual function, set the cooker to High Pressure for 45 minutes (38 minutes at sea level).

2. When the cook time is complete, let the pressure release naturally for 20 minutes; quick release any remaining pressure.

3. Carefully remove the lid and drain the chickpeas. Refrigerate to cool (unless you want to serve this warm, which is good, too).

4. While the chickpeas cool, in a large bowl, stir together the basil, tomatoes, vinegar, garlic powder, and salt. Add the beans, stir to combine, and serve.

PER SERVING: Calories: 396; Total fat: 6g; Saturated fat: 1g; Sodium: 613mg; Carbs: 67g; Fiber: 19g; Protein: 21g

GREEN CHILE CHICKPEAS

BUDGET FRIENDLY • GLUTEN FREE • NUT FREE • SOY FREE

These chickpeas are really versatile, with just the right amount of heat. They make a perfect side dish to Mexican or southwestern-style entrées, and they're also fabulous in tacos or burritos! My favorite way to serve them is in a soft flour taco with lettuce, tomato, and a dollop of Cashew Sour Cream (page 160). Add a small salad and maybe some rice on the side and that's a full (easy) meal. **SERVES 4 TO 6**

PREP TIME:
5 minutes

COOKING SETTING:
Manual, High Pressure for 45 minutes (38 minutes at sea level); Sauté for 4 minutes

RELEASE:
Natural for 20 minutes, then Quick

TOTAL TIME:
1 hour 14 minutes

2 cups dried chickpeas, rinsed

6 cups water

1 small tomato, diced

1 cup diced roasted green chiles (freshly roasted or from a can)

2 teaspoons freshly squeezed lemon juice

1 teaspoon ground cumin

½ teaspoon chili powder, plus more as needed

½ to 1 teaspoon salt

½ teaspoon garlic powder

½ teaspoon red pepper flakes

½ teaspoon smoked paprika

½ teaspoon onion powder

¼ teaspoon dried oregano

¼ teaspoon freshly ground black pepper

1. In your Instant Pot®, combine the chickpeas and water. Lock the lid and turn the steam release handle to Sealing. Using the Manual function, set the cooker to High Pressure for 45 minutes (38 minutes at sea level).

2. When the cook time is complete, let the pressure release naturally for 20 minutes; quick release any remaining pressure.

3. Carefully remove the lid and drain the chickpeas, reserving 1 to 2 tablespoons of the cooking water. Return the chickpeas to the Instant Pot® (be careful, the inner pot will be hot). Stir in the tomato, green chiles, lemon juice, cumin, chili powder, salt, garlic powder, red pepper flakes, paprika, onion powder, oregano, and black pepper. If they're too dry, add the reserved cooking water.

4. On your Instant Pot®, select Sauté Low and cook for 3 to 4 minutes. You may need to turn the Instant Pot® off if anything starts to burn at the bottom. Put the lid back on and turn on the Keep Warm function. Let the chickpeas sit in all that goodness for 5 minutes—then they're ready.

PER SERVING: Calories: 416; Total fat: 6g; Saturated fat: 1g; Sodium: 754mg; Carbs: 71g; Fiber: 18g; Protein: 24g

PREP TIME:
7 minutes

COOKING
SETTING:
Sauté Low
for 6 minutes;
Manual, High
Pressure for
18 minutes
(15 minutes at
sea level)

RELEASE:
Natural for
10 minutes,
then Quick

TOTAL TIME:
41 minutes

MEDITERRANEAN LENTILS

BUDGET FRIENDLY · GLUTEN FREE · NUT FREE · SOY FREE

I always keep lentils on hand so I can easily put together dishes like this. Lentils are inexpensive, easy to store, jam-packed with protein, and they go well with these Mediterranean flavors. Just be sure to use brown or green lentils, not red. Red lentils are split, so they don't stand up to pressure cooking as well. **SERVES 2 TO 4**

---

1 tablespoon olive oil

**1 small sweet or
yellow onion, diced**

1 garlic clove, diced

1 teaspoon dried oregano

½ teaspoon ground cumin

½ teaspoon dried parsley

**½ teaspoon salt, plus
more as needed**

**¼ teaspoon freshly ground black
pepper, plus more as needed**

1 tomato, diced

1 cup brown or green lentils

**2½ cups DIY Vegetable
Stock (page 154), or
store-bought stock**

1 bay leaf

---

1. On your Instant Pot®, select Sauté Low. When the display reads "Hot," add the oil and heat until it shimmers. Add the onion. Cook for 3 to 4 minutes until soft. Turn off the Instant Pot® and add the garlic, oregano, cumin, parsley, salt, and pepper. Cook until fragrant, about 1 minute.

2. Stir in the tomato, lentils, stock, and bay leaf. Lock the lid and turn the steam release handle to Sealing. Using the Manual function, set the cooker to High Pressure for 18 minutes (15 minutes at sea level).

3. When the cook time is complete, let the pressure release naturally for 10 minutes; quick release any remaining pressure.

4. Carefully remove the lid, and remove and discard the bay leaf. Taste and season with more salt and pepper, as needed. If there's too much liquid remaining, select Sauté Medium or High and cook until it evaporates.

VARIATION TIP: These lentils can also be enjoyed as a soup! Simply add another ½ cup of stock before cooking and more vegetables at the start of step 2. Try sliced carrots, additional tomatoes, or chopped zucchini.

PER SERVING: Calories: 426; Total fat: 8g; Saturated fat: 1g; Sodium: 592mg; Carbs: 64g; Fiber: 31g; Protein: 26g

SMOKY BUTTERNUT LENTILS

BUDGET FRIENDLY • GLUTEN FREE • NUT FREE • SOY FREE

The first time I made this recipe, I wanted a smoky lentil side dish with chunks of butternut. I accidently cooked it twice as long as I should have and the lentils and squash were way too soft. The second time the consistency was right, but I just didn't like it as much. That's when I realized the true potential—this amazingly flavorful lentil dish is the best substitute for mashed potatoes (more protein and nutrients for the win). It's a good example of how, sometimes, mistakes can lead to happy endings. **SERVES 4 TO 6**

PREP TIME:
5 minutes

COOKING SETTING:
Sauté Low for 5 minutes; Manual, High Pressure for 10 minutes (9 minutes at sea level)

RELEASE:
Natural for 10 minutes, then Quick

TOTAL TIME:
30 minutes

1 tablespoon olive oil

½ onion, diced

1 garlic clove, minced

1 small butternut squash, peeled and cubed (about 3 cups)

1¾ cups water, or DIY Vegetable Stock (page 154), or store-bought stock

1 cup red lentils, rinsed

1 teaspoon smoked paprika

½ to 1 teaspoon salt

½ teaspoon ground cumin

Pinch chili powder

1. On your Instant Pot®, select Sauté Low. When the display reads "Hot," add the oil and heat until it shimmers. Add the onion. Cook for 2 to 3 minutes, stirring frequently. Turn off the Instant Pot® and add the garlic. Cook for 30 seconds, stirring.

2. Stir in the squash, water, lentils, paprika, salt, cumin, and chili powder. Lock the lid and turn the steam release handle to Sealing. Using the Manual function, set the cooker to High Pressure for 10 minutes (9 minutes at sea level).

3. When the cook time is complete, let the pressure release naturally for 10 minutes; quick release any remaining pressure.

4. Carefully remove the lid and stir. The lentils and butternut will break down quickly—no need to mash. Just stir and, when they're smooth, taste and adjust the seasonings, as needed.

PER SERVING: Calories: 256; Total fat: 4g; Saturated fat: 1g; Sodium: 591mg; Carbs: 43g; Fiber: 17g; Protein: 14g

PREP TIME:
5 minutes

COOKING
SETTING:
Sauté Low
for 4 minutes;
Manual, High
Pressure for
15 minutes
(13 minutes at
sea level)

RELEASE:
Natural for
10 minutes,
then Quick

TOTAL TIME:
34 minutes

SPICY SOUTHWESTERN LENTILS

BUDGET FRIENDLY · GLUTEN FREE · NUT FREE · SOY FREE

Growing up in New Hampshire I wasn't exposed to much in the way of spicy foods. It wasn't until I moved to California in my early twenties that I discovered my love of everything Mexican, southwestern, and Tex-Mex. I especially can't get enough of dishes like these lentils, which are so healthy and easy to make. **SERVES 4 TO 6**

1 tablespoon olive oil

1 small onion, diced

1 or 2 garlic cloves, finely diced

1 bell pepper, any color, diced

2 Roma tomatoes, diced

2 cups DIY Vegetable Stock (page 154), or store-bought stock

1 cup green or brown lentils, rinsed and drained

½ to 1 teaspoon salt, plus more as needed

1 teaspoon ground cumin

1 teaspoon chili powder

1 teaspoon smoked paprika

1 cup well chopped kale

Freshly ground black pepper

1. On your Instant Pot®, select Sauté Low. When the display reads "Hot," add the oil and heat until it shimmers. Add the onion. Sauté for 1 to 2 minutes and then turn off the Instant Pot®. Add the garlic. Cook for about 30 seconds, stirring (don't let it burn).

2. Add the bell pepper, tomatoes, stock, lentils, salt, cumin, chili powder, and paprika. Lock the lid and turn the steam release handle to Sealing. Using the Manual function, set the cooker to High Pressure for 15 minutes (13 minutes at sea level).

3. When the cook time is complete, let the Instant Pot® go into Keep Warm mode and let the pressure release naturally for 10 minutes; quick release any remaining pressure.

4. Carefully remove the lid and stir in the kale, which will wilt after 1 to 2 minutes. Taste and season with salt and pepper, as needed.

PER SERVING: Calories: 247; Total fat: 5g; Saturated fat: 1g; Sodium: 604mg; Carbs: 39g; Fiber: 17g; Protein: 14g

CILANTRO LIME BROWN RICE

BUDGET FRIENDLY • GLUTEN FREE • NUT FREE • SOY FREE

This was the very first recipe I ever created in my Instant Pot®! Its original purpose was for a "Chick'n Fajita" bowl. Since then, this brown rice has played a supporting role in many bowls and burritos. It's so simple, and with so few ingredients, it has become a great go-to grain for me. If you like cilantro, definitely add more, or dice up your favorite spicy pepper and cook it with the rice. **SERVES 4 TO 6**

PREP TIME:
2 minutes

COOKING SETTING:
Manual, High Pressure for 22 minutes (19 minutes at sea level)

RELEASE:
Natural for 10 minutes, then Quick

TOTAL TIME:
34 minutes

2 cups brown rice, rinsed and drained

2½ cups water

⅓ cup fresh cilantro, chopped, plus more as needed

Juice of 1 lime

Zest of 1 lime

Dash ground cumin

Salt

1. In your Instant Pot®, combine the rice and water. Lock the lid and turn the steam release handle to Sealing. Using the Manual function, set the cooker to High Pressure for 22 minutes (19 minutes at sea level).

2. When the cook time is complete, let the pressure release naturally for 10 minutes while the Instant Pot® goes into Keep Warm mode; quick release any remaining pressure.

3. Carefully remove the lid and stir in the cilantro, lime juice and zest, and cumin. Season to taste with salt.

PER SERVING: Calories: 344; Total fat: 3g; Saturated fat: 1g; Sodium: 67mg; Carbs: 72g; Fiber: 3g; Protein: 7g

PREP TIME:
5 minutes

COOKING
SETTING:
Sauté Low
for 5 minutes;
Manual, High
Pressure for
27 minutes
(23 minutes
at sea level)

RELEASE:
Natural for
10, then
Quick

TOTAL TIME:
47 minutes

GARLIC-BUTTER RICE

BUDGET FRIENDLY · GLUTEN FREE · NUT FREE · SOY FREE

Here's a simple way to prepare long-grain brown rice with one of the very best flavors: garlic! While not great for your breath (or for dogs—don't let your pup clean up after this dish), garlic boosts the immune system, and has even been shown to reduce the number, length, and severity of colds. **SERVES 4 TO 6**

2 tablespoons butter-infused olive oil (see tip)

1 small sweet onion, diced

6 to 8 garlic cloves, minced

2 cups long-grain brown rice, rinsed and drained

2½ cups DIY Vegetable Stock (page 154), or store-bought stock

1 teaspoon salt, plus more as needed

Pinch freshly ground black pepper, plus more as needed

1 teaspoon freshly squeezed lemon juice

1 tablespoon vegan butter

Fresh herbs, for garnishing (I like parsley)

1. On your Instant Pot®, select Sauté Low. When the display reads "Hot," add the oil and heat until it shimmers. Add the onion. Sauté for 2 to 3 minutes and then turn off the Instant Pot®. Add the garlic. Cook for about 1 minute, stirring. Add the rice, stock, salt, and pepper, stirring well. Lock the lid and turn the steam release handle to Sealing. Using the Manual function, set the cooker to High Pressure for 27 minutes (23 minutes at sea level).

2. When the cook time is complete, let the pressure release naturally for 10 minutes; quick release any remaining pressure.

3. Carefully remove the lid and stir in the lemon juice and butter. Taste and season with more salt and pepper, as needed. Top with fresh herbs and serve.

SUBSTITUTION TIP: If you can't find butter-infused olive oil, you can use half olive oil and half vegan butter . . . but I really recommend purchasing some of the infused variety online, because the flavor is fantastic. Most brands are vegan, but not all, so double check!

PER SERVING: Calories: 450; Total fat: 13g; Saturated fat: 2g; Sodium: 621mg; Carbs: 77g; Fiber: 4g; Protein: 8g

CITRUS SWEET BASMATI RICE

GLUTEN FREE • NUT FREE • SOY FREE

In my kitchen, I have big bottles of oil and balsamic vinegar I use for everyday cooking—and then I have a set of "fancy" oil and vinegar reserved for special dishes. If you don't already have a fancy balsamic, I encourage you to consider purchasing some Cara Cara Orange-Vanilla white balsamic vinegar online, because it's quite tasty and has so many uses. It goes well with light spring vegetables, so it's good in rice dishes like this (paired with asparagus, carrots, and bell peppers), or as part of a homemade salad dressing. It can lend light, bright flavor to just about anything! **SERVES 4 TO 6**

PREP TIME:
3 minutes

COOKING SETTING:
Manual, High Pressure for 4 minutes (3 minutes at sea level)

RELEASE:
Natural for 5 minutes, then Quick

TOTAL TIME:
12 minutes

2 cups basmati rice, rinsed and drained

2 cups water

1 teaspoon salt, plus more as needed

½ teaspoon garlic powder

¼ cup Cara Cara Orange-Vanilla white balsamic vinegar, or a homemade mixture (see tip)

¼ cup fresh parsley, chopped

Salt

1. In your Instant Pot®, combine the rice, water, salt, and garlic powder. Lock the lid and turn the steam release handle to Sealing. Using the Manual function, set the cooker to High Pressure for 4 minutes (3 minutes at sea level).

2. When the cook time is complete, let the pressure release naturally for 5 minutes; quick release any remaining pressure.

3. Carefully remove the lid and fluff the rice. Stir in the vinegar and parsley. Taste and season with more salt, as needed.

SUBSTITUTION TIP: If you can't find this flavor of vinegar, in a small bowl, whisk plain white balsamic vinegar with just a dash of vanilla extract and 2 tablespoons of freshly squeezed orange juice.

PER SERVING: Calories: 345; Total fat: 1g; Saturated fat: 0g; Sodium: 588mg; Carbs: 76g; Fiber: 2g; Protein: 7g

PREP TIME:
5 minutes

COOKING
SETTING:
Manual, High
Pressure for
4 minutes
(3 minutes at
sea level)

RELEASE:
Natural for
10 minutes,
then Quick

TOTAL TIME:
19 minutes

COCONUT JASMINE RICE

GLUTEN FREE · SOY FREE

Although I'm sure I had eaten it before, I feel like I really discovered—and fell in love with—jasmine rice when I was in Southeast Asia a few years ago. Traveling through Thailand, Cambodia, and Vietnam, I saw the rice being grown and harvested, and I enjoyed it at nearly every meal. This version, cooked with coconut milk, goes perfectly with any Asian dish, especially my Korean Barbecue Chickpea Tacos (page 134). **SERVES 4 TO 6**

2 cups jasmine rice, rinsed and drained

1 (14-ounce) can lite coconut milk

½ cup water

¼ to ½ teaspoon sea salt

1. In your Instant Pot®, combine the rice, coconut milk, water, and salt. Lock the lid and turn the steam release handle to Sealing. Using the Manual function, set the cooker to High Pressure for 4 minutes (3 minutes at sea level).

2. When the cook time is complete, let the pressure release naturally for 10 minutes; quick release any remaining pressure.

3. Carefully remove the lid and fluff the rice. Taste and season with more salt, as needed.

OPTION TIP: To make this into a meal, simply add some frozen veggies after releasing the pressure and let them warm in the rice. You can also top it with baked tofu or peanut sauce.

PER SERVING: Calories: 428; Total fat: 10g; Saturated fat: 9g; Sodium: 245mg; Carbs: 74g; Fiber: 4g; Protein: 6g

JEERA RICE

GLUTEN FREE • NUT FREE • SOY FREE

Indian food tends to be something I'm more likely to order in than make myself . . . except for this rice. I love cumin and use it in a lot of my recipes. Sautéing the spice allows the cumin and cardamom to *bloom* or become amplified, and by using chili oil you add an extra layer of flavor to the rice—a little extra bite, if you will. I buy my chili oil from a local Asian market and always keep a bottle in my fridge. **SERVES 4 TO 6**

PREP TIME:
4 minutes

COOKING SETTING:
Sauté Low for 2 minutes; Manual, High Pressure for 6 minutes (5 minutes at sea level)

RELEASE:
Natural for 10 minutes, then Quick

TOTAL TIME:
22 minutes

1 tablespoon chili oil

2 teaspoons cumin seeds

½ teaspoon ground cardamom

1 teaspoon salt

2 cups basmati rice, rinsed well, drained, and dried

2½ cups water

1. On your Instant Pot®, select Sauté Low. When the display reads "Hot," add the oil and heat until it shimmers. Add the cumin seeds and cardamom. Cook until fragrant, stirring frequently. Add the salt, rice, and water, and stir well. Lock the lid and turn the steam release handle to Sealing. Using the Manual function, set the cooker to High Pressure for 6 minutes (5 minutes at sea level).

2. When the cook time is complete, let the pressure release naturally for 10 minutes; quick release any remaining pressure.

3. Carefully remove the lid and fluff the rice.

PER SERVING: Calories: 372; Total fat: 4g; Saturated fat: 1g; Sodium: 588mg; Carbs: 75g; Fiber: 1g; Protein: 7g

PREP TIME:
5 minutes

COOKING
SETTING:
Sauté Low
for 2 minutes;
Manual, High
Pressure for
5 minutes
(4 minutes at
sea level)

RELEASE:
Natural for
10 minutes,
then Quick

TOTAL TIME:
22 minutes

EASY CHINESE FRIED RICE

NUT FREE

I've found Chinese and other Asian-style restaurants to be very vegan friendly, with tofu options galore (I order a lot of Chinese delivery, so I'm an expert here). The one issue I've discovered is that some don't provide fried rice without egg . . . and what good is sesame tofu without a side of fried rice? The ingredients for this quick dish can be kept in your freezer and pantry and pulled together in the time you'd wait for delivery to arrive at your door! **SERVES 4 TO 6**

1 tablespoon sesame oil

1 small onion, diced

1¾ cups jasmine rice, rinsed and drained

¾ teaspoon ground ginger

¾ teaspoon garlic powder

¼ cup lite soy sauce

1¾ cups water

1½ to 2 cups frozen mixed vegetable (peas, carrots, corn)

1. On your Instant Pot®, select Sauté Low. When the display reads "Hot," add the oil and heat until it shimmers. Add the onion. Cook for 1 minute, stirring frequently. Turn off the Instant Pot® and add the rice, ginger, garlic powder, soy sauce, and water. Lock the lid and turn the steam release handle to Sealing. Using the Manual function, set the cooker to High Pressure for 5 minutes (4 minutes at sea level).

2. When the cook time is complete, turn off the Instant Pot® and let the pressure release naturally for 10 minutes; quick release any remaining pressure.

3. Carefully remove the lid and stir in the frozen vegetables. Rest the lid back on (no need to lock it) and select the Keep Warm function. Let the veggies warm for 3 to 4 minutes before serving.

COOKING TIP: Adding the veggies at the end keeps them from getting soggy!

PER SERVING: Calories: 178; Total fat: 4g; Saturated fat: 1g; Sodium: 913mg; Carbs: 32g; Fiber: 5g; Protein: 5g

ALL-THE-VEGGIES RICE PILAF

BUDGET FRIENDLY • GLUTEN FREE • SOY FREE

This is intended as a side dish, but you could easily add cubes of tofu baked in your favorite sauce (maybe barbecue or agave-sriracha) and make it into a meal. You can also swap onions and mushrooms for double the amount of carrots, and add some zucchini or summer squash, depending on what you're in the mood for or the season. Be creative, there are no rules! **SERVES 4 TO 6**

PREP TIME:
5 minutes

COOKING SETTING:
Sauté Low for 5 minutes; Manual, High Pressure for 3 minutes

RELEASE:
Natural for 15 minutes, then Quick

TOTAL TIME:
28 minutes

1 tablespoon olive oil, or avocado oil

½ sweet onion, chopped

1 carrot, halved lengthwise and sliced

1 celery stalk, sliced

1 cup broccoli florets

½ cup sliced white mushrooms

2 garlic cloves, minced

1 cup basmati rice, rinsed and drained

1 cup DIY Vegetable Stock (page 154), or store-bought stock

Salt

Freshly ground black pepper

½ cup frozen peas

½ cup sliced almonds

1. On your Instant Pot®, select Sauté Low. When the display reads "Hot," add the oil and heat until it shimmers. Add the onion, carrot, celery, broccoli, and mushrooms. Sauté for 2 to 3 minutes, stirring frequently. Add the garlic and turn off the Instant Pot®. Sauté the garlic for 30 seconds, stirring frequently.

2. Stir in the rice and stock and season to taste with salt and pepper. Lock the lid and turn the steam release handle to Sealing. Using the Manual function, set the cooker to High Pressure for 3 minutes.

3. When the cook time is complete, let the pressure release naturally for 15 minutes; quick release any remaining pressure.

4. Carefully remove the lid and stir in the frozen peas. Replace the cover (no need to seal it) and let sit for a few minutes. When ready to serve, stir in the almonds.

PER SERVING: Calories: 307; Total fat: 10g; Saturated fat: 1g; Sodium: 78mg; Carbs: 48g; Fiber: 5g; Protein: 8g

PREP TIME:
7 minutes

COOKING
SETTING:
Manual, High
Pressure for
8 minutes
(7 minutes at
sea level)

RELEASE:
Natural for
10, then
Quick

TOTAL TIME:
25 minutes

COLD QUINOA SALAD WITH FRUIT & PECANS

GLUTEN FREE · SOY FREE

The next time you're headed to a potluck and want to bring something everyone will love, consider this quinoa salad. With all the fruit and nuts, it definitely checks all the nutritional boxes, and it tastes so light and fresh it won't leave anyone feeling too full. You should also consider it for your next meal prep session—it stores well and makes a great packed lunch during the week, especially as it doesn't need to be reheated. **SERVES 4 TO 6**

1 cup quinoa, rinsed

1 cup water

¼ teaspoon salt, plus more as needed

2 apples, unpeeled, cut into large dice

2 tablespoons freshly squeezed lemon juice

1 tablespoon white rice vinegar

½ bunch scallions, green and light green parts, sliced

2 celery stalks, halved lengthwise and chopped

¾ to 1 cup dried cranberries, white raisins, and regular raisins (many stores carry a mix like this in their bulk section)

½ to 1 teaspoon chili powder, plus more as needed

2 tablespoons avocado oil, or walnut oil

Pinch freshly ground black pepper

½ cup fresh cilantro, chopped

½ to 1 cup pecans, chopped

1. In your Instant Pot®, combine the quinoa, water, and salt, and stir. Lock the lid and turn the steam release handle to Sealing. Using the Manual function, set the cooker to High Pressure for 8 minutes (7 minutes at sea level).

2. When the cook time is complete, let the pressure release naturally for 10 minutes; quick release any remaining pressure.

3. Carefully remove the lid and transfer the quinoa to a large bowl. Refrigerate for 5 minutes to cool.

4. In a small resealable container, combine the apples, lemon juice, and vinegar. Cover and shake lightly to coat the apples, then refrigerate.

5. Remove the cooled quinoa from the refrigerator and stir in the scallions, celery, cranberry-raisin mix, chili powder, and oil. Taste and season with more salt and pepper, as needed. Stir the apples and whatever lemon-vinegar juice is in the container into the salad.

6. Add the cilantro and pecans immediately before serving.

MAKE-AHEAD TIP: This salad will last for days in the refrigerator stored in an airtight container; reserve the cilantro and pecans until you're ready to serve.

PER SERVING: Calories: 399; Total fat: 11g; Saturated fat: 1g; Sodium: 169mg; Carbs: 72g; Fiber: 9g; Protein: 9g

PREP TIME:
2 minutes

COOKING
SETTING:
Manual, High
Pressure for
8 minutes
(7 minutes at
sea level)

RELEASE:
Natural
release for
10 minutes,
then Quick

TOTAL TIME:
20 minutes

LEMON PEPPER QUINOA

BUDGET FRIENDLY · GLUTEN FREE · NUT FREE · SOY FREE

This flavorful quinoa makes a spectacular side dish (it's delicious but doesn't steal the spotlight). With just a few additions, it could also be an easy, healthy main dish: Add some of your favorite veggies (asparagus would be great) to cook with the quinoa, or stir them in at the end (try baby spinach). Top with baked tofu and you have yourself a one-bowl meal. As an added bonus, this quinoa freezes nicely—just make sure it's sealed tightly in a food storage bag. **SERVES 4 TO 6**

1½ cups quinoa, rinsed

1½ cups water

½ to 1 teaspoon salt, plus more as needed

½ teaspoon freshly ground black pepper, plus more as needed

¼ teaspoon garlic powder

¼ teaspoon dried basil

1 tablespoon vegan butter

Juice of 1 lemon

Zest of 1 lemon

1. In your Instant Pot®, combine the quinoa, water, salt, pepper, garlic powder, and basil. Lock the lid and turn the steam release handle to Sealing. Using the Manual function, set the cooker to High Pressure for 8 minutes (7 minutes at sea level).

2. When the cook time is complete, let the pressure release naturally for 10 minutes; quick release any remaining pressure.

3. Carefully remove the lid and stir in the butter, lemon juice, and zest. Taste and season with more salt and pepper, as needed.

PER SERVING: Calories: 261; Total fat: 7g; Saturated fat: 1g; Sodium: 618mg; Carbs: 41g; Fiber: 5g; Protein: 9g

MUSHROOM & LEEK RISOTTO

GLUTEN FREE • NUT FREE • SOY FREE

This risotto is rich and creamy and the mushrooms are cooked to soft perfection. The whole dish basically melts in your mouth. Risotto is equally at home in a five-star restaurant or on your couch—it's elevated comfort food! I prefer baby bellas, but any mushroom will work. **SERVES 4 TO 6**

PREP TIME:
7 minutes

COOKING SETTING:
Sauté Low for 5 minutes; Manual, High Pressure for 8 minutes (7 minutes at sea level)

RELEASE:
Quick

TOTAL TIME:
20 minutes

4 tablespoons vegan butter, divided

1 leek, white and lightest green parts only, halved and sliced, rinsed well

12 ounces baby bella mushrooms, sliced

2 garlic cloves, minced

1 cup Arborio rice, rinsed and drained

2¾ cups DIY Vegetable Stock (page 154), or store-bought stock

1 teaspoon dried thyme

½ teaspoon salt, plus more as needed

Juice of ½ lemon

Freshly ground black pepper

Chopped fresh parsley, for garnishing

1. On your Instant Pot®, select Sauté Low. When the display reads "Hot," add 2 tablespoons of butter to melt. Add the leek and mushrooms. Sauté for about 2 minutes, stirring frequently. Add the garlic. Cook for about 30 seconds, stirring—turn off the Instant Pot® if it starts to burn. Add the rice and toast it for 1 minute. Turn off the Instant Pot®.

2. Stir in the stock, thyme, and salt. Lock the lid and turn the steam release handle to Sealing. Using the Manual function, set the cooker to High Pressure for 8 minutes (7 minutes at sea level).

3. When the cook time is complete, quick release the pressure.

4. Carefully remove the lid and stir in the lemon juice and remaining 2 tablespoons of vegan butter. Taste and season with more salt and pepper, as needed. Garnish with fresh parsley.

PER SERVING: Calories: 311; Total fat: 12g; Saturated fat: 2g; Sodium: 437mg; Carbs: 46g; Fiber: 3g; Protein: 6g

PREP TIME:
4 minutes

COOKING
SETTING:
Sauté Low
for 4 minutes;
Manual, High
Pressure for
8 minutes
(7 minutes at
sea level)

RELEASE:
Quick

TOTAL TIME:
16 minutes

CREAMY VEGGIE RISOTTO

BUDGET FRIENDLY · GLUTEN FREE · NUT FREE · SOY FREE

Before the Instant Pot®, making risotto meant standing at your stove stirring. And stirring some more. You couldn't risk walking away or the rice might burn. It was exhausting! Now you just have to sauté for a couple minutes, then you're free to go read a book or play with your dog until it's done cooking. It's basically a risotto miracle. **SERVES 4 TO 6**

---

2 tablespoons olive oil

½ sweet onion, diced

1 garlic clove, minced

1 bunch asparagus tips, cut into 1-inch pieces

2¾ cups DIY Vegetable Stock (page 154), or store-bought stock

1 cup Arborio rice, rinsed and drained

1 cup sugar snap peas, rinsed, tough ends removed

1 teaspoon dried thyme

½ teaspoon salt, plus more as needed

¼ teaspoon freshly ground black pepper

Pinch red pepper flakes

2 tablespoons vegan butter

Juice of ½ lemon

1½ to 2 cups fresh baby spinach, torn

---

1. On your Instant Pot®, select Sauté Low. When the display reads "Hot," add the oil and heat until it shimmers. Add the onion. Cook for about 2 minutes, stirring frequently. Turn off the Instant Pot® and stir in the garlic and asparagus, cooking for 30 seconds.

2. Add the stock, rice, peas, thyme, salt, black pepper, and red pepper flakes, stirring well. Lock the lid and turn the steam release handle to Sealing. Using the Manual function, set the cooker to High Pressure for 8 minutes (7 minutes at sea level).

3. When the cook time is complete, quick release the pressure.

4. Carefully remove the lid and stir in the butter, lemon juice, and spinach, being gentle so as not to tear the snap peas. Taste and season with more salt, as needed.

SUBSTITUTION TIP: Use your favorite veggies in this risotto! If they'll stand up to cooking, include them with the rice. If it's something lighter (like the spinach) stir in at the very end.

PER SERVING: Calories: 309; Total fat: 13g; Saturated fat: 2g; Sodium: 375mg; Carbs: 43g; Fiber: 4g; Protein: 5g

Sweet Potato &
Black Bean Tacos

7

VEGETABLE
MAINS

PREP TIME:
10 minutes

COOKING
SETTING:
Manual, High
Pressure for
2 minutes

RELEASE:
Quick

TOTAL TIME:
12 minutes

RED THAI CURRY CAULIFLOWER

BUDGET FRIENDLY · GLUTEN FREE · SOY FREE

Conquer your take-out cravings with this easy Thai curry. Serve it over rice, enjoy it on its own, or turn up the nutrient meter by stirring in your favorite greens at the end. This curry gets more flavorful the longer it sits, so leftovers make great lunches. Of course, it's so delicious that it's hard not to eat it all the first time around! **SERVES 4 TO 6**

1 (14-ounce) can full-fat coconut milk

½ to 1 cup water

2 tablespoons red curry paste

1 teaspoon garlic powder

1 teaspoon salt, plus more as needed

½ teaspoon ground ginger

½ teaspoon onion powder

¼ teaspoon chili powder (Thai is great, or cayenne pepper)

1 bell pepper, any color, thinly sliced

1 small to medium head cauliflower, cut into bite-size pieces (3 to 4 cups)

1 (14-ounce) can diced tomatoes and liquid

Freshly ground black pepper

Cooked rice or other grain, for serving (optional)

1. In your Instant Pot®, stir together the coconut milk, water, red curry paste, garlic powder, salt, ginger, onion powder, and chili powder. Add the bell pepper, cauliflower, and tomatoes, and stir again. Lock the lid and turn the steam release handle to Sealing. Using the Manual function, set the cooker to High Pressure for 2 minutes.

2. When the cook time is complete, quick release the pressure.

3. Carefully remove the lid and give the whole thing a good stir. Taste and season with more salt and pepper, as needed. Serve with rice or another grain (if using).

INGREDIENT TIP: Full-fat coconut milk helps make this curry rich and thick, but you can use the lighter-calorie lower-fat version, if you prefer.

PER SERVING: Calories: 349; Total fat: 31g; Saturated fat: 26g; Sodium: 943mg; Carbs: 18g; Fiber: 6g; Protein: 5g

POLENTA & KALE

BUDGET FRIENDLY · GLUTEN FREE · NUT FREE · SOY FREE

There are so many ways to enjoy polenta, and I would argue this is one of the best. The polenta is creamy and rich (thank you vegan butter and nutritional yeast!), and *ohmygoodness* that garlicky kale! Whenever someone tells me they don't like kale, I ask if they've had it sautéed in oil with garlic and salt and, of course, they say no. Because if they had, they would know that they do, in fact, LOVE kale! So if you have anyone in your life who is iffy on polenta or kale, have them try a bowl of this goodness. **SERVES 4 TO 6**

PREP TIME:
5 minutes

COOKING SETTING:
Sauté Low for 3 minutes; Manual, High Pressure for 20 minutes (17 minutes at sea level)

RELEASE:
Natural release for 15 minutes, then Quick

TOTAL TIME:
43 minutes

1 tablespoon olive oil

2 bunches kale, stemmed, leaves chopped

3 or 4 garlic cloves, minced

1 teaspoon salt, divided, plus more as needed

1 cup polenta

1 quart DIY Vegetable Stock (page 154), or store-bought stock

2 tablespoons nutritional yeast

2 to 3 tablespoons vegan butter

Freshly ground black pepper

1. On your Instant Pot®, select Sauté Low. When the display reads "Hot," add the oil and heat until it shimmers. Add the kale, garlic, and ½ teaspoon of salt. Cook for about 2 minutes, stirring frequently so nothing burns, until the kale is soft and the garlic is fragrant. (You can always turn off the Instant Pot® if it gets too hot.) Transfer the garlicky kale to a bowl and set aside.

2. In your Instant Pot®, combine the polenta, stock, and remaining ½ teaspoon of salt. Lock the lid and turn the steam release handle to Sealing. Using the Manual function, set the cooker to High Pressure for 20 minutes (17 minutes at sea level).

3. When the cook time is complete, let the pressure release naturally for 15 minutes; quick release any remaining pressure.

4. Carefully remove the lid and stir well (some liquid may have accumulated on top of the polenta). Add the nutritional yeast and butter along with any additional salt and pepper. Serve in bowls topped with the kale.

PER SERVING: Calories: 329; Total fat: 13g; Saturated fat: 2g; Sodium: 729mg; Carbs: 46g; Fiber: 5g; Protein: 10g

PREP TIME:
10 minutes

COOKING
SETTING:
Manual, Low
Pressure for
2 minutes

RELEASE:
Natural for
8 minutes,
then Quick

TOTAL TIME:
20 minutes

BUTTERNUT MAC 'N' CHEESE

SOY FREE

There are lots of vegan mac and cheese recipes out there that use store-bought nondairy cheeses (I should know, I have a few on my blog!). Those are great, but sometimes you want one made with wholesome ingredients you can feel good about. This recipe meets those requirements and is still highly crave-able. Win-win! If you want to add a little green, mix in some frozen peas at the end. **SERVES 6**

1 cup raw cashews, soaked in water for at least 3 to 4 hours, or overnight, drained and rinsed well

2 cups cooked cubed butternut squash (I buy frozen cubes and thaw them in advance)

⅓ cup nutritional yeast

2 tablespoons freshly squeezed lemon juice

1 teaspoon Dijon mustard

2 to 2½ teaspoons salt

⅛ teaspoon ground nutmeg

4½ cups water, divided

1 (16-ounce) box pasta (I like small shells or campanelle)

1 cup nondairy milk, plus more as needed

Freshly ground black pepper

1. In a high-speed blender or food processor, combine the cashews, squash, nutritional yeast, lemon juice, mustard, salt, nutmeg, and 2 cups of water. Blend until smooth (the longer you soaked the cashews, the quicker this will be). Pour the cashew mixture into your Instant Pot®.

2. Pour the remaining 2½ cups of water into the blender and swish it around to capture any remaining cashew mixture. Add that to the Instant Pot® as well, along with the pasta. Lock the lid and turn the steam release handle to Sealing. Using the Manual function, set the cooker to Low Pressure for 2 minutes.

3. When the cook time is complete, turn off the Instant Pot® and let the pressure release naturally for 8 minutes; quick release any remaining pressure.

4. Carefully remove the lid and stir in the milk, adding as much as needed to make it nice and creamy. Taste and season with more salt and pepper, as needed.

INGREDIENT TIP: Packaged nutritional yeast can be found in the baking aisle of most grocery stores, and in the bulk section of health stores.

INGREDIENT TIP: Did you know butternut squash is technically a fruit? It's true, and it's because the squash contains seeds. It is also low in fat, high in fiber, and provides some serious potassium and vitamin B_6!

PER SERVING: Calories: 520; Total fat: 14g; Saturated fat: 2g; Sodium: 654mg; Carbs: 78g; Fiber: 10g; Protein: 23g

PREP TIME:
5 minutes

COOKING
SETTING:
Sauté Low
for 4 minutes;
Manual, High
Pressure for
4 minutes
(3 minutes at
sea level)

RELEASE:
Natural for
5 minutes,
then Quick

TOTAL TIME:
18 minutes

SWEET POTATO & BLACK BEAN TACOS

NUT FREE • SOY FREE

Whether you're celebrating Taco Tuesday, Margarita Monday, or just plain old Wednesday, these tacos are just the thing you need. They're filling, delicious, and not too spicy. They're also really nutritious—full of protein from the beans and vitamins A, B_6, and C from the sweet potatoes. The filling reheats well. The only question now is, flour or corn tortillas? **SERVES 4 TO 6**

1 to 2 tablespoons olive oil

½ sweet onion, diced

1 large sweet potato, diced

1 red bell pepper, diced

1 garlic clove, minced

1 tomato, diced

1 (15-ounce) can black beans, rinsed and drained

1 canned chipotle pepper in adobo sauce, diced

1 to 2 teaspoons adobo sauce from the can

1 to 2 teaspoons chili powder

½ teaspoon salt

½ teaspoon ground cumin

½ cup DIY Vegetable Stock (page 154), or store-bought stock

1 tablespoon freshly squeezed lime juice

Zest of 1 lime

Corn or flour tortillas, for serving

1 avocado, peeled, pitted, and mashed

¼ cup fresh cilantro, chopped

Cashew Sour Cream (page 160), for serving (optional)

Garden Salsa (page 159), for serving (optional)

Sliced jalapeño peppers, for serving (optional)

Sliced red cabbage, for serving (optional)

1. On your Instant Pot®, select Sauté Low. When the display reads "Hot," add the oil and heat until it shimmers. Add the onion. Cook for 1 minute, stirring. Add the sweet potato and bell pepper. Cook for 1 minute, stirring so nothing burns. Turn off the Instant Pot® and add the garlic. Cook for 30 seconds to 1 minute, stirring.

2. Add the tomato, black beans, chipotle, adobo sauce, chili powder, salt, cumin, stock, and lime juice. Lock the lid and turn the steam release handle to Sealing. Using the Manual function, set the cooker to High Pressure for 4 minutes (3 minutes at sea level).

3. When the cook time is complete, turn off the Instant Pot® and let the pressure release naturally for 5 minutes; quick release any remaining pressure.

4. Carefully remove the lid. If there is too much liquid in the inner pot, select Sauté Low again and cook for 1 to 2 minutes, stirring constantly (it gets hot fast!).

5. Stir in the lime zest. Serve in the tortillas, topped with mashed avocado and cilantro and anything else your heart desires.

INGREDIENT TIP: Chipotle peppers in adobo are a common ingredient in Mexican dishes and can be found in the Mexican or ethnic aisle of most grocery stores. Most recipes call for a small amount, and you can freeze the remainder for another recipe.

PER SERVING: Calories: 369; Total fat: 16g; Saturated fat: 2g; Sodium: 420mg; Carbs: 51g; Fiber: 15g; Protein: 12g

PREP TIME:
10 minutes

COOKING
SETTING:
Manual, High
Pressure for
45 minutes
(38 minutes
at sea level);
Sauté Low
for 8 to
10 minutes

RELEASE:
Natural for
15 minutes,
then Quick

TOTAL TIME:
1 hour
20 minutes

CHICKPEA KALE KORMA

SOY FREE

Korma is my favorite of the Indian curries because it's so flavorful without being spicy hot. This is a simple yet nutritious dish I like to make during my meal prep session, and then reheat during the week for lunches. Why? Because the flavors get even better as the beans and kale sit in that delicious sauce. It's great served over rice, although I tend to enjoy it most on its own—the kale and beans are plenty filling. **SERVES 4 TO 6**

---

1 cup dried chickpeas, rinsed

1 to 2 cups water

½ cup cashews, soaked in water overnight, drained and rinsed well

2 Roma tomatoes, quartered

3 garlic cloves, peeled

½-inch piece fresh ginger, peeled

1 (14-ounce) can lite coconut milk

1 teaspoon garam masala

1 teaspoon curry powder

½ to 1 teaspoon salt

½ teaspoon ground cumin

½ teaspoon ground coriander

½ teaspoon ground cardamom

½ teaspoon ground turmeric

½ teaspoon onion powder

¼ teaspoon freshly ground black pepper

1 bunch kale, leaves torn from stems and rinsed

Hot cooked rice, for serving (optional)

---

1. In your Instant Pot®, combine the chickpeas and enough water to cover. Lock the lid and turn the steam release handle to Sealing. Using the Manual function, set the cooker to High Pressure for 45 minutes (38 minutes at sea level).

2. When the cook time is complete, let the pressure release naturally for 15 minutes; quick release any remaining pressure.

3. Carefully remove the lid. Drain the chickpeas and return them to the Instant Pot®.

4. In a high-speed blender or food processor, combine the cashews, tomatoes, garlic, and ginger. Blend until smooth. Add the coconut milk and pulse a few more times to combine. Add this purée to the chickpeas along with the garam masala, curry powder, salt, cumin, coriander, cardamom, turmeric, onion powder, pepper, and kale.

5. On your Instant Pot®, select Sauté Low. Simmer for 8 to 10 minutes until the kale and beans have absorbed the flavor. Serve with rice, if desired.

SUBSTITUTION TIP: Kale is my go-to, but you can easily substitute spinach, collard greens, Swiss chard, or any other greens you have on hand.

PER SERVING: Calories: 442; Total fat: 21g; Saturated fat: 10g; Sodium: 377mg; Carbs: 52g; Fiber: 11g; Protein: 18g

PREP TIME:
5 minutes

COOKING
SETTING:
Sauté Low
for 4 minutes;
Manual, High
Pressure for
8 minutes
(7 minutes
at sea level);
Sauté Low
again for
5 minutes

RELEASE:
Natural
release for
10 minutes,
then Quick

TOTAL TIME:
32 minutes

DECONSTRUCTED CABBAGE ROLLS

BUDGET FRIENDLY · GLUTEN FREE · NUT FREE

When a traditional dish is "deconstructed" it usually means the ingredients have been separated and artfully arranged (usually in a very expensive restaurant), or that they've all been combined into casserole form. Personally, I like casserole-type meals (I'm a one-bowl kinda girl), and I love cooking big batches that leave me with plenty of leftovers—both of which this recipe accomplishes. **SERVES 6 TO 8**

FOR THE TEMPEH

1 tablespoon olive oil

1 (8-ounce) package unflavored tempeh, crumbled

2 teaspoons Montreal steak seasoning

2 teaspoons vegan Worcestershire sauce

2 garlic cloves, minced

1 bay leaf

½ onion, diced

FOR THE DECONSTRUCTED CABBAGE ROLLS

1 cup basmati rice, rinsed and drained

1 cup water

½ teaspoon salt, plus more as needed

1½ cups DIY Vegetable Stock (page 154), or store-bought stock

1 head cabbage, thinly sliced

6 ounces tomato paste

½ teaspoon paprika

¼ teaspoon freshly ground black pepper, plus more as needed

Pinch cayenne pepper, plus more as needed

¼ cup chopped fresh parsley

TO MAKE THE TEMPEH

On your Instant Pot®, select Sauté Low. When the display reads "Hot," add the oil and heat until it shimmers. Add the tempeh, Montreal steak seasoning, Worcestershire sauce, garlic, bay leaf, and onion. Cook for 3 to 4 minutes, stirring frequently. Transfer to a bowl and set aside.

TO MAKE THE DECONSTRUCTED CABBAGE ROLLS

1. In your Instant Pot®, combine the rice, water, and salt. Lock the lid and turn the steam release handle to Sealing. Using the Manual function, set the cooker to High Pressure for 8 minutes (7 minutes at sea level).

2. When the cook time is complete, let the pressure release naturally for 10 minutes; quick release any remaining pressure.

3. Carefully remove the lid and fluff the rice. Add the stock, cabbage, tomato paste, paprika, black pepper, and cayenne. Select Sauté Low again and cook for 4 to 5 minutes until the cabbage softens a little. Turn off the Instant Pot®, remove and discard the bay leaf, and stir in the parsley. Taste and season with more salt and pepper, as needed.

PER SERVING: Calories: 276; Total fat: 7g; Saturated fat: 1g; Sodium: 455mg; Carbs: 43g; Fiber: 5g; Protein: 13g

PREP TIME:
10 minutes

COOKING
SETTING:
Manual, High
Pressure for
4 minutes
(3 minutes
at sea level);
Sauté Low for
10 minutes

RELEASE:
Natural for
5 minutes,
then Quick

TOTAL TIME:
29 minutes

ASIAN-STYLE COCONUT RICE & VEGGIES

BUDGET FRIENDLY · GLUTEN FREE

This nontraditional Chinese dish is a little bit sweet, a little bit savory, and completely full of vegetables. It's a fun alternative to fried rice, especially if you're a fan of coconut. If you've never worked with Chinese five-spice before, it's a combination of the five spices most commonly used in Chinese cuisine. It's used in savory dishes, desserts, and even cocktails! There are different variations, but all have a similar flavor. **SERVES 4 TO 6**

1 cup jasmine rice, rinsed and drained

1 cup water

1 teaspoon salt

½ teaspoon ground ginger

1 tablespoon sesame oil

1 large carrot, sliced

1 small onion, diced

1 cup chopped bok choy

1 cup sugar snap peas, rinsed, tough ends removed

2 garlic cloves, minced

8 ounces white button mushrooms, sliced

1 (8-ounce) can sliced water chestnuts, drained

1 (14-ounce) can lite coconut milk

1 teaspoon Chinese five-spice

1 teaspoon soy sauce

1. In your Instant Pot®, combine the rice, water, salt, and ginger. Lock the lid and turn the steam release handle to Sealing. Using the Manual function, set the cooker to High Pressure for 4 minutes (3 minutes at sea level).

2. When the cook time is complete, let the pressure release naturally for 5 minutes; quick release any remaining pressure.

3. Carefully remove the lid and fluff the rice. Transfer to a bowl and set aside.

4. On your Instant Pot®, select Sauté Low. When the display reads "Hot," add the oil and heat until it shimmers. Add the carrot, onion, bok choy, snap peas, garlic, mushrooms, and water chestnuts. Sauté for 2 to 3 minutes.

5. Stir in the coconut milk, five-spice powder, soy sauce, and cooked rice. Simmer for 5 to 6 minutes more, stirring occasionally, until the coconut milk is reduced.

INGREDIENT TIP: Frozen snap peas are great to keep in your freezer (I stock up when they're on sale!), but if you're using fresh peas, be sure to rinse them well and remove any thick or hard ends.

PER SERVING: Calories: 418; Total fat: 13g; Saturated fat: 9g; Sodium: 738mg; Carbs: 70g; Fiber: 4g; Protein: 10g

PREP TIME:
12 minutes

COOKING
SETTING:
Manual, High
Pressure for
8 minutes
(7 minutes at
sea level)

RELEASE:
Natural for
5 minutes,
then Quick

TOTAL TIME:
25 minutes

LAYERED MEXICAN CASSEROLE

BUDGET FRIENDLY · GLUTEN FREE · SOY FREE

I'm not sure how authentic this Mexican casserole is, but I can certainly vouch for how delicious it is! There's definitely a little heat in there (especially if you use my Red Hot Enchilada Sauce [page 157]!), which is easy to adjust by using more or less chili powder. The mashed sweet potatoes add a nice counterbalance to keep it from being a scorcher. You can also cool it off a little bit with some Cashew Sour Cream (page 160) or avocado. **SERVES 4 TO 6**

Nonstick cooking spray, for preparing the springform pan

2 cups mashed sweet potatoes (about 2 potatoes)

1¼ cups Red Hot Enchilada Sauce (page 157), or 1 (10-ounce) can, divided

1 tablespoon freshly squeezed lime juice

½ to 1 teaspoon chili powder

½ teaspoon garlic powder

½ teaspoon onion powder

1 (15-ounce) can black beans, rinsed and drained

1 (10-ounce) can diced tomatoes with green chilies, drained

½ cup sliced scallion, green and light green parts, divided

¼ cup frozen sweet corn

8 or 9 taco-size, gluten-free corn tortillas

Vegan cheese shreds, for topping (optional)

½ cup water

Cashew Sour Cream (page 160), for serving

Poblano Cheeze Sauce (page 158), for serving

Sliced avocado, for serving

1. Lightly coat the bottom and sides of a 7-inch springform pan with nonstick spray and set aside.

2. In a medium bowl, stir together the mashed sweet potatoes, 1 cup of enchilada sauce, the lime juice, chili powder, garlic powder, and onion powder.

3. In another medium bowl, stir together the black beans, tomatoes and green chilies, ¼ cup of scallion, the corn, and 3 tablespoons of enchilada sauce.

4. To build the casserole, spread the remaining 1 tablespoon of enchilada sauce on the bottom of the prepared pan. Add a layer of tortillas, torn as needed to get full coverage. Don't be afraid to overlap. Layer on one-third of the sweet potato mixture. Using a slotted spoon, top the sweet potato later with one-third of the black bean mixture. Repeat the tortilla layer, sweet potato layer, and black bean layer two more times. Top with the remaining ¼ cup of scallion. If using vegan cheese shreds, add them now.

5. Spray a piece of aluminum foil with nonstick spray and cover the pan tightly.

6. Pour the water into the Instant Pot® and place a trivet into the inner pot. Set the covered casserole on top of the trivet. Lock the lid and turn the steam release handle to Sealing. Using the Manual function, set the cooker to High Pressure for 8 minutes (7 minutes at sea level).

7. When the cook time is complete, let the pressure release naturally for 5 minutes; quick release any remaining pressure.

8. Carefully remove the lid and the trivet and casserole from the Instant Pot®. Set aside on a heat-resistant surface. Remove the foil and let cool for at least 5 minutes before releasing the sides of the pan. Plate and add desired toppings before serving.

PER SERVING: Calories: 381; Total fat: 5g; Saturated fat: 1g; Sodium: 456mg; Carbs: 72g; Fiber: 16g; Protein: 15g

PREP TIME:
1 hour

COOKING
SETTING:
Sauté Low for
20 minutes

RELEASE:
None

TOTAL TIME:
1 hour
20 minutes

MOO GOO GAI PAN

GLUTEN FREE · NUT FREE

I order a lot of Chinese food, but I tend to stick to items I know will be vegan friendly. Ordering with a tablet from my couch is convenient, but it makes asking questions a little more difficult. So to satisfy my cravings for this Chinese stir-fry without risking unknown ingredients, I've perfected this version I can make myself. I also like that it's a totally different way to use the Instant Pot® (without pressure)—just another reminder of how versatile it is. **SERVES 4 TO 6**

FOR THE MARINADE

2 tablespoons DIY Vegetable Stock (page 154), or store-bought stock

2 tablespoons lite soy sauce

1 tablespoon sesame oil

1 garlic clove, minced

½-inch piece fresh ginger, peeled and grated

FOR THE STIR-FRY

1 (14-ounce) block firm tofu, pressed for least 1 hour, but overnight is best (the longer it's pressed, the more flavor it will soak up from the marinade), chopped into bite-size cubes

1 tablespoon sesame oil

8 ounces white mushrooms, sliced

1 cup sugar snap peas, rinsed, tough ends removed

1 carrot, sliced into matchsticks

1 garlic clove, minced

1-inch piece fresh ginger, peeled and grated

1 cup DIY Vegetable Stock (page 154), or store-bought stock

2 tablespoons soy sauce

1 (8-ounce) can sliced water chestnuts, drained

1 (8-ounce) can bamboo shoots, drained

1 tablespoon cornstarch

⅓ cup water

Hot cooked rice or noodles, for serving (optional)

TO MAKE THE MARINADE

In a small bowl, whisk the stock, soy sauce, oil, garlic, and ginger. Set aside.

TO MAKE THE STIR-FRY

1. In a shallow dish, combine the tofu cubes and marinade. Cover the dish and let sit for at least 30 minutes.

2. On your Instant Pot®, select Sauté Low. When the display reads "Hot," add the oil and heat until it shimmers. Add the marinated tofu. Cook for 8 to 10 minutes, using tongs to turn the tofu carefully.

3. Turn off the Instant Pot® and add the mushrooms, snap peas, carrot, garlic, ginger, stock, soy sauce, water chestnuts, and bamboo shoots. Using a large spoon, stir well.

4. On your Instant Pot®, select Sauté Low again. Cover the pot with a tempered glass lid (either one you purchased for the Instant Pot® or another that fits) and simmer for 5 minutes, stirring occasionally.

5. In a small bowl, whisk the cornstarch and water. Add this slurry to the pot. Simmer, uncovered, for 5 minutes more, or until the sauce thickens. Serve over rice or noodles (if using).

TECHNIQUE TIP: I mentioned a few accessories for your Instant Pot® in chapter 1 (see page 6) and a tempered glass lid was one. It's very handy in recipes like this, when you need to keep an eye on what is cooking.

PER SERVING: Calories: 274; Total fat: 12g; Saturated fat: 2g; Sodium: 928mg; Carbs: 33g; Fiber: 4g; Protein: 14g

PREP TIME:
20 minutes

COOKING SETTING:
Sauté Low for 4 minutes; Manual, High Pressure for 25 minutes (21 minutes at sea level)

RELEASE:
Natural release for 15 minutes, then Quick

TOTAL TIME:
1 hour 4 minutes

VEGETABLE LASAGNA

BUDGET FRIENDLY

Lasagna was one of the first dishes I learned to make and, although I perfected my technique over the years, it's never been this easy! This dish is also a good example of why a springform pan is a great addition to your Instant Pot® accessories collection. It keeps layered casseroles like this one neat and tidy, and cleanup is a snap. **SERVES 4 TO 6**

FOR THE TOFU RICOTTA

1 (14-ounce) container firm tofu, pressed for 5 to 10 minutes

⅓ cup nutritional yeast

3 tablespoons nondairy milk, plus more as needed

2 teaspoons dried oregano

1½ teaspoons onion powder

1½ teaspoons garlic powder

1 teaspoon dried basil

1 teaspoon salt, plus more as needed

Freshly ground black pepper

FOR THE LASAGNA

Nonstick cooking spray, for preparing the springform pan

2 tablespoons plus 1 cup water, divided

1 small zucchini, diced (about 1 cup)

½ sweet onion, diced

1 garlic clove, minced

½ teaspoon salt

Pinch red pepper flakes

6 to 8 dried lasagna noodles

4 cups Butternut Basil Red Sauce (page 155), or favorite red pasta sauce, divided

8 fresh basil leaves, chopped

TO MAKE THE TOFU RICOTTA

In a large bowl, combine the tofu, nutritional yeast, milk, oregano, onion powder, garlic powder, basil, and salt, and season to taste with pepper. Using a wooden spoon or potato masher, break down the tofu and stir until everything is combined and the mixture is smooth. Stir in additional milk, by the tablespoon, if you need more moisture. Alternatively, combine the ingredients in a food processor and pulse a few times until smooth.

TO MAKE THE LASAGNA

1. Lightly coat the bottom and sides of a 7-inch springform pan with nonstick spray. Set aside.

2. On your Instant Pot®, select Sauté Low. When the display reads "Hot," add 2 tablespoons of water to heat. Add the zucchini, onion, garlic, salt, and red pepper flakes. Cook for 2 to 3 minutes until they begin to soften. Turn off the Instant Pot® and remove the veggies.

3. Place a layer of lasagna noodles in the pot, breaking them to get maximum coverage. Spread 1 cup of sauce over the noodles and top with half the veggie mix and half the ricotta. Repeat. Finally, add a third layer of lasagna noodles and another 1 cup of sauce. (You should have 1 cup left.) Lightly coat a piece of aluminum foil with nonstick spray and tightly cover the pan.

4. Pour 1 cup of water into the Instant Pot® and place a trivet into the inner pot. Set the covered lasagna on top of the trivet. Lock the lid and turn the steam release handle to Sealing. Using the Manual function, set the cooker to High Pressure for 25 minutes (21 minutes at sea level).

5. When the cook time is complete, let the pressure release naturally for 15 minutes; quick release any remaining pressure.

6. Carefully remove the lid and the trivet and pan from the Instant Pot® and remove the foil. Let the lasagna cool for at least 5 minutes before releasing the sides of the pan (it helps to leave it on the trivet during this time). The longer you wait to release, the easier it will be to slice.

7. Top with fresh basil and the remaining sauce.

TECHNIQUE TIP: I use a full batch of tofu ricotta in my lasagna because I like it a little gooey and messy. If you're using vegan cheese in yours (or if you just want a super neat lasagna), scale back and only use half to three-fourths of the ricotta.

PER SERVING: Calories: 414; Total fat: 8g; Saturated fat: 1g; Sodium: 1239mg; Carbs: 64g; Fiber: 12g; Protein: 32g

PREP TIME:
10 minutes

COOKING
SETTING:
Sauté Low
for 6 minutes;
Manual, High
Pressure for
3 minutes

RELEASE:
Natural for
5 minutes,
then Quick

TOTAL TIME:
24 minutes

MUSHROOM KALE STROGANOFF

BUDGET FRIENDLY

Stroganoff, traditionally made with beef, is a dish I never had until I was vegan! I actually saw it on a menu and thought, "I must veganize this!"– and so I did. I kept the mushrooms because, in addition to being full of nutrition, they're delicious. They also make a great meat substitute because they're so hearty and toothsome. I also added kale because, well, I felt like the dish needed something green. The kale also keeps it from being too rich. **SERVES 4 TO 6**

1 tablespoon olive oil

1 sweet onion, diced

2 garlic cloves, minced

1 pound baby bella mushrooms, sliced

1 tomato, diced

1 teaspoon smoked paprika

1 bay leaf

½ teaspoon salt, plus more as needed

3 cups dried campanelle pasta, or similar shape

3¼ cups DIY Vegetable Stock (page 154), or store-bought stock

1 cup Cashew Sour Cream (page 160)

3 cups kale leaves, rinsed and torn into bite-size pieces

1. On your Instant Pot®, select Sauté Low. When the display reads "Hot," add the oil and heat until it shimmers. Add the onion. Sauté for 2 minutes, stirring frequently. Turn off the Instant Pot® and add the garlic. Cook for 1 minute, stirring.

2. Add the mushrooms, tomato, paprika, bay leaf, and salt. Let sit for 2 to 3 minutes.

3. Stir in the pasta and stock. Lock the lid and turn the steam release handle to Sealing. Using the Manual function, set the cooker to High Pressure for 3 minutes.

4. When the cook time is complete, let the pressure release naturally for 5 minutes; quick release any remaining pressure.

5. Carefully remove the lid, and remove and discard the bay leaf. If there is excess liquid in the pot, select Sauté Low again and cook for 1 to 2 minutes, stirring frequently, to evaporate some of it. Turn off the pot and stir in the sour cream and kale. Let sit for 1 to 2 minutes while the kale wilts. Taste and season with more salt, as needed.

INGREDIENT TIP: If you have store-bought vegan sour cream, you can substitute that, but don't skip it—it's a very important component of this dish.

PER SERVING: Calories: 616; Total fat: 22g; Saturated fat: 4g; Sodium: 608mg; Carbs: 85g; Fiber: 7g; Protein: 22g

PREP TIME:
10 minutes

COOKING
SETTING:
Oven for
30 minutes
(26 minutes
at sea level);
Manual, High
Pressure for
5 minutes
(4 minutes at
sea level)

RELEASE:
Natural for
10 minutes,
then Quick

TOTAL TIME:
55 minutes

THANKSGIVING BOWL

GLUTEN FREE · NUT FREE

I'm that nerd who starts planning the Thanksgiving menu in September and is humming carols by the middle of October. I LOVE THE HOLI-DAYS! I won't apologize. During the rest of the year, when I start to crave my favorite season, I make this Thanksgiving bowl. I use baked tofu, my own Mushroom Gravy (page 161), and canned cranberry sauce I stockpile like a deranged squirrel to recreate the big feast, on a smaller, healthier level. **SERVES 4 TO 6**

FOR THE BAKED TOFU

Nonstick cooking spray, for preparing the baking sheet

1 (14-ounce) package firm tofu, pressed overnight, halved shortways, then again through the middle to get 4 thin rectangles

1 tablespoon Montreal chicken seasoning

¼ teaspoon dried thyme

Few pinches rubbed sage

Salt

Freshly ground black pepper

FOR THE BOWLS

4 red potatoes, quartered

1 teaspoon salt

1 to 2 cups water

2 to 4 tablespoons vegan butter

¼ to ½ cup nondairy milk

Salt

Freshly ground black pepper

1 cup frozen corn

1 (14-oz) can cranberry sauce, jellied or whole berry

1 to 2 cups Mushroom Gravy (page 161)

½ cup crispy fried onions (like French's)

TO MAKE THE BAKED TOFU

1. Preheat oven to 400°F. Lightly coat a baking sheet with nonstick spray.

2. Lay the tofu slices on the baking sheet.

3. In a small bowl, stir together the Montreal chicken seasoning, thyme, and sage. Season to taste with salt and pepper, keeping in mind there's salt in the Montreal seasoning. Spritz the top of the tofu lightly with the nonstick spray and sprinkle some seasoning mix on top.

4. Bake for 15 minutes (13 minutes at sea level). Spray the seasoned side of the tofu first (so it doesn't stick) with cooking spray. Flip and spray the unseasoned side (now facing up) and add more seasoning mix. Bake for 15 minutes more (13 minutes more at sea level).

5. When it's done baking, cut the tofu into cubes and toss it in the remaining seasoning mix.

TO MAKE THE BOWLS

1. In your Instant Pot®, combine the potatoes, salt, and just enough water to cover them. Lock the lid and turn the steam release handle to Sealing. Using the Manual function, set the cooker to High Pressure for 5 minutes (4 minutes at sea level).

2. When the cook time is complete, let the pressure release naturally for 10 minutes; quick release any remaining pressure.

3. Carefully remove the lid and drain out the water. Add the butter and milk to the pot, and season the potatoes to taste with the salt and pepper. Mash the potatoes in the inner pot.

4. Stir in the corn, cover the pot, and turn on the Keep Warm function. Cover the pot and let sit for 2 to 3 minutes.

5. Assemble the bowls with potatoes and corn on the bottom, topped with the tofu. I like to do half of the next layer with cranberry sauce and half with gravy, with crispy onions on the very top.

PER SERVING: Calories: 585; Total fat: 26g; Saturated fat: 4g; Sodium: 1456mg; Carbs: 78g; Fiber: 8g; Protein: 15g

PREP TIME:
10 minutes

COOKING
SETTING:
Sauté Low for
11 minutes

RELEASE:
None

TOTAL TIME:
21 minutes

MUCHO BURRITOS

Everyone loves burritos, and I'm so glad that vegans can partake, too. With the spicy-smoky tofu, rich Poblano Cheeze Sauce (page 158), and cool Cashew Sour Cream (page 160), these burritos are missing exactly *nothing*. It's all there—the flavor, the heat, the delicious gooey mess of the best handheld meal ever invented. I'm especially proud of the chipotle adobo tofu. It reminds me a lot of the vegan tofu offered at a certain burrito chain, and I hope you'll love it, too. **SERVES 6 TO 8**

1 tablespoon roasted walnut oil

1 (14-ounce) container firm tofu, pressed for at least 1 hour, or overnight if possible, and crumbled

2 canned chipotle peppers in adobo sauce

1 to 2 teaspoons adobo sauce from the can

1 teaspoon ground cumin

½ teaspoon salt

½ teaspoon garlic powder

½ teaspoon freshly squeezed lime juice

Pinch freshly ground black pepper

1 bell pepper, any color, sliced

1 small onion, sliced

¼ cup DIY Vegetable Stock (page 154), or store-bought stock

6 to 8 burrito-size tortillas

2 cups Cilantro Lime Brown Rice (page 93)

1 (16-ounce) can chili beans, drained but not rinsed

Garden Salsa (page 159), or store-bought salsa of choice, for filling

2 cups Poblano Cheeze Sauce (page 158)

Cashew Sour Cream (page 160), for filling (optional)

Sliced avocado, for filling (optional)

1. On your Instant Pot®, select Sauté Low. When the display reads "Hot," add the oil and heat until it shimmers. Add the tofu crumbles, chipotle peppers, adobo sauce, cumin, salt, garlic powder, lime juice, and pepper. Cook for 2 to 3 minutes. Add the bell pepper and onion. Cook for 2 minutes more. If you need additional liquid, add 1 to 2 tablespoons of water.

2. Add the stock and simmer, stirring occasionally, for 4 to 5 minutes until the liquid is cooked out. Turn off the Instant Pot®.

3. To build your burritos, layer the tortillas with rice, tofu mixture, chili beans (using a slotted spoon so you don't get too much chili sauce), salsa, poblano cheeze sauce, and other fillings, as desired.

SERVING TIP: If you'd prefer to skip the tortillas, simply double the rice and serve as bowls instead.

PER SERVING: Calories: 460; Total fat: 20g; Saturated fat: 4g; Sodium: 1225mg; Carbs: 53g; Fiber: 11g; Protein: 22g

PREP TIME:
10 minutes

COOKING
SETTING:
Sauté Low
for 6 minutes;
Manual, High
Pressure for
2 minutes

RELEASE:
Quick

TOTAL TIME:
18 minutes

TEMPEH SLOPPY JANES

NUT FREE

Did you eat sloppy Joes as a child? Extra points if yours came out of a can! I'm sure we all enjoyed them back then, but one of the benefits of being an adult is we have total say over what we eat. We can choose healthier and more compassionate options, and I like calling these sloppy Janes, not Joes, to highlight that difference. This is a fun, hearty sandwich you can feel good about serving—whether you're pairing it with salad or fries. **SERVES 4 TO 6**

1 tablespoon olive oil

1 (8-ounce) package unflavored tempeh

1 teaspoon smoked paprika

½ teaspoon salt, plus more as needed

About 2 cups Refried Pinto Beans (page 86) or 1 (15-ounce) can vegan refried beans

1 (10-ounce) can diced tomatoes with green chilies, with liquid

½ cup DIY Vegetable Stock (page 154), or store-bought stock

2 tablespoons vegan Worcestershire sauce

1 tablespoon Dijon mustard

½ teaspoon garlic powder

1 or 2 pinches chili powder

Freshly ground black pepper

¼ cup quick cook oats

4 to 6 buns or rolls, for serving

Sliced onion, for serving

Sliced bell pepper, for serving

Pickles, for serving

Vegan cheese, for serving

Barbecue sauce, for serving

1. On your Instant Pot®, select Sauté Low. When the display reads "Hot," add the oil and heat until it shimmers. Crumble in the tempeh and add the paprika and salt. Cook for 4 to 5 minutes, stirring occasionally. Turn off the Instant Pot®.

2. Add the refried beans, tomatoes and green chilies, stock, Worcestershire sauce, mustard, garlic powder, and chili powder, and season to taste with pepper. Lock the lid and turn the steam release handle to Sealing. Using the Manual function, set the cooker to High Pressure for 2 minutes.

3. When the cook time is complete, quick release the pressure.

4. Carefully remove the lid and stir in the oats. There will likely be too much liquid; if so, select Sauté Medium and cook, uncovered, for 2 to 3 minutes, or until the extra liquid evaporates. Serve on buns, topped as desired.

INGREDIENT TIP: My preference is to layer the onions and peppers on top of my sandwich, but if you prefer to dice them and mix them into the sloppy Janes, add them during step 4. That will allow them to cook a little, without becoming too soft. If you're adding vegan cheese, that's the best time for that as well.

PER SERVING: Calories: 339; Total fat: 13g; Saturated fat: 2g; Sodium: 722mg; Carbs: 43g; Fiber: 6g; Protein: 19g

PREP TIME:
10 minutes

COOKING SETTING:
Manual, High Pressure for 45 minutes (38 minutes at sea level); Sauté Low for 7 minutes

RELEASE:
Natural for 15 minutes, then Quick

TOTAL TIME:
1 hour 17 minutes

KOREAN BARBECUE CHICKPEA TACOS

NUT FREE

Korean food has become quite popular where I live, but many Korean recipes aren't traditionally vegan friendly, so I've had to make my own! Korean barbecue sauce is spicy, sweet, and savory—it's basically everything. I love to make my own, and I've used it in countless dishes, from pan-fried seitan to pizza to stir-fries. These tacos are an easy introduction, and I'm pretty sure you'll soon be using the sauce as much as I do! **SERVES 4 TO 6**

1 cup dried chickpeas, rinsed

1 to 2 cups plus 3 tablespoons water, divided

3 tablespoons cornstarch

2 to 3 tablespoons gochujang (Korean hot pepper paste)

⅓ cup packed light brown sugar

⅓ cup soy sauce

2 tablespoons hot chili oil

2 teaspoons rice wine vinegar

½ teaspoon onion powder

½ teaspoon garlic powder

2 cups pineapple chunks

1 teaspoon sriracha, plus more as needed

6 to 8 taco shells

1. In your Instant Pot®, combine the chickpeas with enough water to cover. Lock the lid and turn the steam release handle to Sealing. Using the Manual function, set the cooker to High Pressure for 45 minutes (38 minutes at sea level).

2. When the cook time is complete, let the pressure release naturally for 15 minutes; quick release any remaining pressure.

3. Carefully remove the lid and pour the contents into a colander to drain. Return the chickpeas to the inner pot.

4. In a small bowl, whisk the cornstarch and 3 tablespoons of water. Set aside.

5. On your Instant Pot®, select Sauté Low.

6. To the chickpeas, add the gochujang, brown sugar, soy sauce, chili oil, vinegar, onion powder, and garlic powder. Cook until it starts to bubble. Stir in the cornstarch slurry. Simmer for 4 to 5 minutes more, stirring frequently, until the sauce thickens and the chickpeas are nice and coated.

7. In a medium bowl, stir together the pineapple and sriracha. Taste before adding more sauce. Fill the taco shells with the chickpeas and top with the pineapple.

SUBSTITUTION TIP: Many grocery stores (and most Asian markets) carry premade Korean barbecue sauce, which makes an easy substitution. Use 1 to 1¼ cups for this recipe.

PER SERVING: Calories: 592; Total fat: 18g; Saturated fat: 3g; Sodium: 1389mg; Carbs: 93g; Fiber: 12g; Protein: 15g

PREP TIME:
8 minutes

COOKING
SETTING:
Sauté Low
for 7 minutes;
Manual, High
Pressure for
4 minutes
(3 minutes at
sea level)

RELEASE:
Quick

TOTAL TIME:
19 minutes

GERMAN VEGETABLE SALAD

BUDGET FRIENDLY · GLUTEN FREE · NUT FREE

I'm a rule follower by nature, except when it comes to food. I enjoy pushing boundaries and trying crazy combinations. I love the flavors of German potato salad, but I wanted to beef it up (so to speak) and see if it could be an entire meal. So I added tempeh bacon and Brussels sprouts (Protein! Green veggies!) and now we have a hearty, filling meal with plenty of nutrition. If you choose to serve it as a side, it serves 6 to 8 people. **SERVES 4 TO 6**

FOR THE DRESSING

½ cup apple cider vinegar

½ cup DIY Vegetable Stock (page 154), or store-bought stock

2 teaspoons Dijon mustard

½ to 1 teaspoon salt

½ teaspoon garlic powder

FOR THE SALAD

1½ tablespoons olive oil

1 (8-ounce) package unflavored tempeh, chopped into bite-size pieces

1½ teaspoons smoked paprika

½ teaspoon salt, plus more as needed

¼ teaspoon garlic powder

1½ pounds red potatoes, chopped

2 cups Brussels sprouts, ends trimmed, loose or yellowed outer leaves removed, rinsed with cold water, and any large Brussels sprouts halved

1 small red onion, sliced

2 bay leaves

¼ cup chopped fresh parsley

Freshly ground black pepper

TO MAKE THE DRESSING

In a medium bowl, whisk the vinegar, stock, mustard, salt, and garlic powder until well combined. Set aside.

TO MAKE THE SALAD

1. On your Instant Pot®, select Sauté Low. When the display reads "Hot," add the oil and heat until it shimmers. Add the tempeh, paprika, salt, and garlic powder. Cook for 5 to 6 minutes, stirring occasionally. Transfer to a bowl and set aside.

2. Now add the potatoes, Brussels sprouts, red onion, and bay leaves to the Instant Pot®. Pour the dressing over the vegetables. Lock the lid and turn the steam release handle to Sealing. Using the Manual function, set the cooker to High Pressure for 4 minutes (3 minutes at sea level).

3. When the cook time is complete, quick release the pressure.

4. Carefully remove the lid, and remove and discard the bay leaves. Stir in the tempeh and parsley. Taste and season with more salt and pepper, as needed. There will be some liquid left in the bottom, which is perfect for spooning over the salad when it's served. If there's too much liquid for your taste, select Sauté Low again and cook for 2 to 3 minutes more.

INGREDIENT TIP: Ever wonder how these tiny cabbages got their name? Although they've been cultivated since the fifth century, it was in Brussels, Belgium, that they gained widespread popularity, sometime in the thirteenth century.

PER SERVING: Calories: 322; Total fat: 12g; Saturated fat: 2g; Sodium: 933mg; Carbs: 41g; Fiber: 8g; Protein: 16g

PREP TIME:
5 minutes

COOKING
SETTING:
Manual, High
Pressure for
1 minute;
Sauté Low for
4 minutes

RELEASE:
Quick

TOTAL TIME:
10 minutes

KIMCHI PASTA

SOY FREE

I'm no culinary genius, but I really enjoy combining favorite aspects of different cuisines. This recipe, for example, brings together the long-term relationship I'm in with Italian food and my newfound appreciation for Korean food! If you've never had kimchi, it's a popular Korean side dish made of fermented vegetables—it's spicy and delicious. It's also an excellent source of vitamins B_6, C, and K. **SERVES 4 TO 6**

---

8 ounces dried small pasta

2⅓ cups DIY Vegetable Stock (page 154), or store-bought stock

2 garlic cloves, minced

½ red onion, sliced

½ to 1 teaspoon salt

1¼ cups kimchi, with any larger pieces chopped

½ cup Cashew Sour Cream (page 160)

---

1. In your Instant Pot®, combine the pasta, stock, garlic, red onion, and salt. Lock the lid and turn the steam release handle to Sealing. Using the Manual function, set the cooker to High Pressure for 1 minute.

2. When the cook time is complete, quick release the pressure.

3. Carefully remove the lid. On your Instant Pot®, select Sauté Low. Stir in the kimchi. Simmer for 3 to 4 minutes. Stir in the sour cream, and serve!

INGREDIENT TIP: Most health food stores and many grocery stores carry jars of premade kimchi. It's also widely available at Asian markets, but be aware that many varieties are made with fish and aren't vegan. I personally prefer a brand called Mother-in-Law's.

PER SERVING: Calories: 283; Total fat: 5g; Saturated fat: 1g; Sodium: 936mg; Carbs: 49g; Fiber: 2g; Protein: 10g

GOBI MASALA

BUDGET FRIENDLY · GLUTEN FREE · NUT FREE · SOY FREE

This simple dish is from North India, where it is traditionally served with rice or roti, an Indian flatbread. It's light yet filling, and none of the flavors are overwhelming. I also like it because the ingredients are all easy to find and use in other recipes—if you like Indian cuisine, none of them will go to waste, collecting dust in your spice cabinet. The fact that the main ingredient is cauliflower (gobi) makes this dish even more of a winner in my book, because cauliflower is one of my favorite veggies, and it's very nutritious. It contains at least some of nearly every single vitamin and mineral humans need! **SERVES 4 TO 6**

PREP TIME:
5 minutes

COOKING SETTING:
Sauté Low for 6 minutes; Manual, High Pressure for 1 minute

RELEASE:
Quick

TOTAL TIME:
12 minutes

1 tablespoon olive oil

1 teaspoon cumin seeds

1 white onion, diced

1 garlic clove, minced

1 head cauliflower, chopped

1 tablespoon ground coriander

1 teaspoon ground cumin

½ teaspoon garam masala

½ teaspoon salt

1 cup water

Hot cooked rice, for serving (optional)

1. On your Instant Pot®, select Sauté Low. When the display reads "Hot," add the oil and heat until it shimmers. Add the cumin seeds. Cook for 30 seconds, stirring nearly constantly. Add the onion. Cook for 2 to 3 minutes, still stirring! Turn off the Instant Pot® and add the garlic. Cook for about 30 seconds, stirring frequently.

2. Add the cauliflower, coriander, cumin, garam masala, salt, and water. Lock the lid and turn the steam release handle to Sealing. Using the Manual function, set the cooker to High Pressure for 1 minute.

3. When the cook time is complete, quick release the pressure.

4. Carefully remove the lid and serve with hot rice (if using).

PER SERVING: Calories: 97; Total fat: 4g; Saturated fat: 1g; Sodium: 356mg; Carbs: 14g; Fiber: 6g; Protein: 5g

PREP TIME:
10 minutes

COOKING SETTING:
Sauté Low for 4 minutes; Manual, High Pressure for 20 minutes (17 minutes at sea level)

RELEASE:
Natural for 15 to 20 minutes, then Quick

TOTAL TIME:
54 minutes

HOPPIN' JOHN

BUDGET FRIENDLY • NUT FREE • SOY FREE

This dish is traditionally served in the South on New Year's Day to make the New Year prosperous and full of luck. I cannot guarantee this recipe will bring you anything other than a full and happy belly (especially since this isn't a totally traditional recipe), but don't let that stop you. Lucky or not, a tasty meal full of grains, legumes, and veggies is a great way for anyone to kick off the New Year—or even just a new week! **SERVES 4 TO 6**

---

1 tablespoon olive oil

1 sweet onion, diced

1 red bell pepper, diced

2 tomatoes, chopped

1 teaspoon chili powder

1 teaspoon vegan Worcestershire sauce

½ teaspoon garlic powder

½ teaspoon dried thyme

½ teaspoon salt

¼ teaspoon freshly ground black pepper

1 cup dried black-eyed peas, rinsed

3¼ cups DIY Vegetable Stock (page 154), or store-bought stock

1 cup frozen peas

2 cups cooked brown rice

2 to 3 cups chopped kale

---

1. On your Instant Pot®, select Sauté Low. When the display reads "Hot," add the oil and heat until it shimmers. Add the onion and bell pepper. Cook for 2 to 3 minutes, stirring occasionally. Turn off the Instant Pot® and add the tomatoes, chili powder, Worcestershire sauce, garlic powder, thyme, salt, pepper, black-eyed peas, and stock. Lock the lid and turn the steam release handle to Sealing. Using the Manual function, set the cooker to High Pressure for 20 minutes (17 minutes at sea level).

2. When the cook time is complete, let the pressure release naturally for about 20 minutes; quick release any remaining pressure.

3. Carefully remove the lid and stir in the frozen peas, rice, and kale. Give them a minute or two to warm, and enjoy.

PER SERVING: Calories: 386; Total fat: 5g; Saturated fat: 1g; Sodium: 368mg; Carbs: 70g; Fiber: 13g; Protein: 17g

SIMPLE TOMATO BASIL PASTA

BUDGET FRIENDLY · NUT FREE · SOY FREE

This truly is a simple pasta dish, yet so full of flavor! If you're someone who doesn't like a lot of sauce on their pasta, this is for you. It's also a lifesaver when you just don't have sauce (or the ingredients to make your own) on hand. The tomatoes break down while the pasta cooks so you'll get a little with each bite, and the sweet basil smells and tastes delightful—I can't help but smile every time I eat it. **SERVES 2**

PREP TIME:
3 minutes

COOKING SETTING:
Manual, High Pressure for 2 minutes

RELEASE:
Quick

TOTAL TIME:
5 minutes

2 cups dried campanelle or similar pasta

1¾ cups DIY Vegetable Stock (page 154), or store-bought stock

½ teaspoon salt, plus more as needed

2 tomatoes, cut into large dice

1 or 2 pinches red pepper flakes

½ teaspoon dried oregano

½ teaspoon garlic powder

10 to 12 fresh sweet basil leaves

Freshly ground black pepper

1. In your Instant Pot®, stir together the pasta, stock, and salt. Drop the tomatoes on top (do not stir). Lock the lid and turn the steam release handle to Sealing. Using the Manual function, set the cooker to High Pressure for 2 minutes.

2. When the cook time is complete, quick release the pressure.

3. Carefully remove the lid and stir in the red pepper flakes, oregano, and garlic powder. If there's more than a few tablespoons of liquid in the bottom, select Sauté Low and cook for 2 to 3 minutes until it evaporates.

4. When ready to serve, chiffonade the basil and stir it in. Taste and season with more salt and pepper, as needed.

TECHNIQUE TIP: Chiffonade is a fancy way of saying you should pile the leaves into a neat stack and roll them up. Then, with a sharp knife, simply slice them into thin ribbons.

PER SERVING: Calories: 416; Total fat: 2g; Saturated fat: 0g; Sodium: 484mg; Carbs: 84g; Fiber: 5g; Protein: 15g

Brandy-Soaked
Cheater
Cherry Pie

8

TREATS, SWEETS &
DESSERTS

PREP TIME:
5 minutes

COOKING
SETTING:
Manual, High
Pressure for
8 minutes
(7 minutes at
sea level)

RELEASE:
Natural
for 10 to
12 minutes,
then Quick

TOTAL TIME:
25 minutes

BOURBON APPLE CRISP

NUT FREE · SOY FREE

A deliciously adult twist on an old classic! There is just a hint of bourbon flavor, enough to make this treat a little more special. My family loves this recipe—especially my little brother—so it's a common request. Lucky for me it's so easy to make! I find that the best apples are crisp and tart, such as Honeycrisp, Pink Lady, Braeburns, or Jonagolds. Whichever variety you choose, make sure they're firm and fresh. **SERVES 4**

---

5 apples, peeled and cut into thick slices

2 tablespoons maple syrup

2 tablespoons ground cinnamon

½ teaspoon ground nutmeg

Salt

¼ cup water

¼ cup bourbon

4 tablespoons vegan butter

¾ cup old-fashioned oats

¼ cup all-purpose flour

½ cup packed light brown sugar

---

1. In your Instant Pot®, stir together the apples, maple syrup, cinnamon, nutmeg, and pinch of salt. Cover the apples with the water and bourbon.

2. In a medium microwave-safe bowl, microwave the butter until just barely melted. Add the oats, flour, brown sugar, and ½ teaspoon of salt. Stir to combine. Spoon the oat mixture over the apples, getting as much coverage as possible. Lock the lid and turn the steam release handle to Sealing. Using the Manual function, set the cooker to High Pressure for 8 minutes (7 minutes at sea level).

3. When the cook time is complete, let the pressure release naturally for 10 to 12 minutes; quick release any remaining pressure. Turn off the Instant Pot®.

4. Carefully remove the lid and let the crisp rest for a few minutes to thicken before serving.

INGREDIENT TIP: If you don't want to use bourbon, simply add another ¼ cup of water.

PER SERVING: Calories: 476; Total fat: 13g; Saturated fat: 2g; Sodium: 184mg; Carbs: 86g; Fiber: 10g; Protein: 3g

VANILLA POACHED PEARS WITH CARAMEL SAUCE

NUT FREE • SOY FREE

Most pears will work in this recipe, but I've found the Bosc variety stands up best to the cooking process. When it's time to plate your impressive dessert, slice a tiny bit off the bottom of the pears so they'll stand up. And while they're perfect with just the caramel sauce, if you want to take this dessert to the next level, add a scoop of vanilla ice cream, or even a cupcake. There's no limit to how decadent this can get! **SERVES 4**

PREP TIME:
7 minutes

COOKING SETTING:
Sauté Low for 2 minutes; Manual, High Pressure for 3 minutes

RELEASE:
Quick

TOTAL TIME:
12 minutes

3 cups water

2 cups white wine

2 cups sugar

1 whole vanilla bean, split and scraped

1 cinnamon stick

4 Bosc pears, ripe but not soft

1 lemon, halved

1 batch Easy Caramel Sauce (page 151), warmed

1. On your Instant Pot®, select Sauté Low. When the display reads "Hot," add the water, white wine, sugar, vanilla bean and seeds, and cinnamon stick, stirring well. Cook for 1 to 2 minutes, or until the sugar dissolves completely. Cancel Sauté and select Keep Warm.

2. Gently peel the pears. If presentation is important, keep the stems intact. Rub the pears with the lemon halves to prevent browning and add the pears to the Instant Pot®. Lock the lid and turn the steam release handle to Sealing. Using the Manual function, set the cooker to High Pressure for 3 minutes.

3. When the cook time is complete, quick release the pressure.

4. Carefully remove the lid and remove the pears. Set aside to cool. Save the sauce and pour it over the pears once cooled. Serve, warm or at room temperature, topped with caramel sauce.

PER SERVING: Calories: 520; Total fat: 9g; Saturated fat: 9g; Sodium: 60mg; Carbs: 107g; Fiber: 7g; Protein: 1g

PREP TIME:
7 minutes

COOKING
SETTING:
Manual, High
Pressure for
3 minutes;
Sauté
Medium
for 5 to
10 minutes

RELEASE:
Natural for
10 minutes,
then Quick

TOTAL TIME:
20 minutes

FRESH FRUIT COMPOTE

GLUTEN FREE · NUT FREE · SOY FREE

There are far too many possible uses for this compote for me to list, but let's give it a shot. Serve it atop waffles or pancakes, or with your favorite yogurt. Use it in Fruity Quinoa & Granola Bowls (page 20), or mix a spoonful into your Maple Morning Millet (page 28). It would also be amazing as part of any dessert, from vegan cheesecake to cupcakes to a plain ol' bowl of nondairy vanilla ice cream. **MAKES 4 CUPS**

6 cups mixed berries (I like a 2:1 ratio of strawberries to blueberries)

1½ cups sugar

¼ cup freshly squeezed orange juice

1. In your Instant Pot®, combine the berries, sugar, and orange juice. Lock the lid and turn the steam release handle to Sealing. Using the Manual function, set the cooker to High Pressure for 3 minutes.

2. When the cook time is complete, turn off the Instant Pot® and let the pressure release naturally for 10 minutes; quick release any remaining pressure.

3. Carefully remove the lid. Select Sauté Medium. Stir the berry mixture and cook for 5 to 10 minutes (depending on how much liquid there is) so some of the excess liquid evaporates. Switch to Low if it's spattering too much. When you've reached the desired consistency, let the compote cool a bit before enjoying.

PER SERVING (½ CUP): Calories: 179; Total fat: 0g; Saturated fat: 0g; Sodium: 0mg; Carbs: 47g; Fiber: 2g; Protein: 1g

CINNAMON-VANILLA APPLESAUCE

BUDGET FRIENDLY · GLUTEN FREE · NUT FREE · SOY FREE

I love applesauce because it's delicious enough to feel like a treat, yet nutritious enough to be a healthy snack. Stir some into a bowl of granola or serve it on top of vegan vanilla ice cream—the pairing possibilities are endless! If you're wondering what type of apples are best to use, my recommendations are Fuji and Golden Delicious because they cook down quickly and easily. I also like Honeycrisp and Granny Smiths for their flavor. And, leave the peels on for the extra fiber—you won't be able to tell after they've been blended. **SERVES 6 TO 8**

PREP TIME:
10 minutes

COOKING SETTING:
Manual, High Pressure for 5 minutes (4 minutes at sea level)

RELEASE:
Natural for 10 minutes, then Quick

TOTAL TIME:
25 minutes

3 pounds apples, cored and quartered, no need to peel

⅓ cup water

1 teaspoon vanilla extract

1 teaspoon ground cinnamon, plus more as needed

1 teaspoon freshly squeezed lemon juice

½ teaspoon salt

1. In your Instant Pot®, combine the apples, water, vanilla, cinnamon, lemon juice, and salt. Lock the lid and turn the steam release handle to Sealing. Using the Manual function, set the cooker to High Pressure for 5 minutes (4 minutes at sea level).

2. When the cook time is complete, let the pressure release naturally for 10 minutes; quick release any remaining pressure.

3. Carefully remove the lid. Using an immersion blender, blend the applesauce until smooth. Taste and add more cinnamon, as desired.

FREEZER TIP: Pack into freezer-safe food storage bags for when you need a snack. Just thaw in your refrigerator. Applesauce also works well as an egg substitute for baking, so it's versatile to keep on hand.

PER SERVING: Calories: 61; Total fat: 0g; Saturated fat: 0g; Sodium: 195mg; Carbs: 13g; Fiber: 3g; Protein: 0g

PREP TIME:
5 minutes

COOKING
SETTING:
Porridge for
20 minutes
(17 minutes at
sea level)

RELEASE:
Natural for
10 minutes,
then Quick

TOTAL TIME:
35 minutes

CINNAMON COCONUT RICE PUDDING

SOY FREE

My discovery of rice pudding happens to have coincided with my purchase of the Instant Pot®, and I can't believe what I was missing all these years! It's so creamy and delicious, and you can adjust the ingredients and toppings to cure nearly any craving. I love how quick and versatile this pudding is (especially in the Instant Pot®). My favorite toppings are coconut flakes, maple syrup, and raisins. **SERVES 4 TO 6**

---

1 cup jasmine rice, rinsed and drained

1 (14-ounce) can full-fat coconut milk

1¾ to 2 cups water (depending on how creamy you want your pudding)

2 teaspoons ground cinnamon

1½ teaspoons vanilla extract

½ teaspoon ground nutmeg

½ to 1 teaspoon salt

¼ cup sugar

Nondairy milk, to thin after cooking

Maple syrup, for topping

Coconut flakes, for topping

Raisins, for topping

---

1. In your Instant Pot®, combine the rice, coconut milk, water, cinnamon, vanilla, nutmeg, salt, and sugar. If needed, whisk to break down any chunks from the canned coconut milk. Lock the lid and turn the steam release handle to Sealing. Select the Porridge function. This will automatically cook for 20 minutes (17 minutes at sea level).

2. When the cook time is complete, let the pressure release naturally for 10 minutes; quick release any remaining pressure.

3. Carefully remove the lid and stir in the milk if you want a thinner pudding. Keep in mind it will thicken as it cools, so if you're planning to reheat it later you'll likely need more milk.

PER SERVING: Calories: 504; Total fat: 29g; Saturated fat: 25g; Sodium: 600mg; Carbs: 57g; Fiber: 5g; Protein: 6g

STICKY RICE & FRESH FRUIT

GLUTEN FREE · SOY FREE

I was lucky enough to try this dish in Thailand, and searching out new spots for my daily sticky rice fix soon became part of my routine. It's traditionally served with mango, but any fruit will do; I recommend really ripe peaches, and even canned fruit will serve in a pinch. **SERVES 4**

PREP TIME:
5 minutes

COOKING SETTING:
Manual, High Pressure for 14 minutes (12 minutes at sea level)

RELEASE:
Natural for 10 to 12 minutes, then Quick

TOTAL TIME:
31 minutes

¾ to 1 cup full-fat coconut milk

¼ cup sugar

½ teaspoon salt

2¼ cups water, divided

1 cup sweet rice, rinsed and drained

Sliced fresh fruit, for serving

1. In a small saucepan over low heat, make the coconut sauce by combining the coconut milk, sugar, and salt. Cook for 2 to 3 minutes, stirring frequently—don't let it boil—until the sugar dissolves. Remove from the heat.

2. Pour 1 cup of water into the Instant Pot® and place a trivet into the inner pot. In a medium glass or stainless steel bowl, combine the remaining 1¼ cups water and the rice, ensuring the rice is completely covered. Place the bowl atop the trivet. Lock the lid and turn the steam release handle to Sealing. Using the Manual function, set the cooker to High Pressure for 14 minutes (12 minutes at sea level).

3. When the cook time is complete, let the pressure release naturally for 10 to 12 minutes; quick release any remaining pressure.

4. Carefully remove the lid and add half the coconut sauce. Cover the cooker and let sit for at least 5 minutes so the rice absorbs the liquid.

5. Top each serving with fruit and additional coconut sauce.

PER SERVING: Calories: 230; Total fat: 14g; Saturated fat: 13g; Sodium: 300mg; Carbs: 26g; Fiber: 2g; Protein: 2g

PREP TIME:
35 minutes

COOKING SETTING:
Sauté Low for 15 minutes

RELEASE:
None

TOTAL TIME:
50 minutes

BRANDY-SOAKED CHEATER CHERRY PIE

BUDGET FRIENDLY • NUT FREE • SOY FREE

I'm a big fan of cherry pie. I'm actually a fan of most pies but don't like to bake, so I don't partake very often. When I do commit to putting in that level of effort, it is almost always for cherry pie. Until, that is, I decided to become a cheater. I realized that the filling is the easy part, and by combining those delicious cherries with fillo shells from the freezer section of my grocery store, most of the work is already done! **SERVES 6 TO 8**

2 pounds cherries, pitted

⅓ cup brandy

⅔ cup sugar

3 tablespoons cornstarch

Pinch salt

Juice of ½ lime

2 (1.9-ounce) boxes mini fillo shells

1. In a large bowl, combine the cherries and brandy. Let soak for 30 minutes, stirring occasionally.

2. On your Instant Pot®, select Sauté Low. When the display reads "Hot," pour the cherries and whatever liquid is at the bottom of the bowl into the inner pot. Stir in the sugar, cornstarch, salt, and lime juice. Cook for 10 to 15 minutes, stirring frequently so nothing burns, until thickened.

3. Let cool for a few minutes before spooning the filling into the fillo shells.

INGREDIENT TIP: Frozen cherries are fine to use; thaw them completely before soaking.

PER SERVING: Calories: 288; Total fat: 3g; Saturated fat: 1g; Sodium: 74mg; Carbs: 61g; Fiber: 3g; Protein: 4g

EASY CARAMEL SAUCE

BUDGET FRIENDLY · SOY FREE

Yes, making caramel sauce truly is this easy! Honestly, the most difficult part of this recipe is going to the store to buy the condensed coconut milk. Once that part is behind you, you're only about an hour away from a thick, rich, sweet, and creamy caramel sauce that (in my opinion) tastes far superior to caramel made with cow's milk. Why? The coconut! It's also easy to play with the flavor by adding a little salt or vanilla. **SERVES 4 TO 6**

1 (11-ounce) can sweetened condensed coconut milk

1 cup water

1 teaspoon coarse sea salt (optional)

PREP TIME:
5 minutes

COOKING SETTING:
Manual, High Pressure for 45 minutes (38 minutes at sea level)

RELEASE:
Natural release for 20 minutes

TOTAL TIME:
1 hour 10 minutes

1. Peel the label off the can and place the can on a trivet and into your Instant Pot®. Pour in the water. Lock the lid and turn the steam release handle to Sealing. Using the Manual function, set the cooker to High Pressure for 45 minutes (38 minutes at sea level).

2. When the cook time is complete, let the pressure release naturally for about 20 minutes, or until the pin drops.

3. Carefully remove the lid. Wearing oven mitts, carefully remove the can and trivet. Set aside until cool enough to handle.

4. Once cooled, open the can and pour the caramel sauce into a glass jar for storage. If separation occurs, whisk for 1 minute or so. For a salted caramel, stir in the sea salt.

PER SERVING: Calories: 281; Total fat: 9g; Saturated fat: 9g; Sodium: 56mg; Carbs: 49g; Fiber: 0g; Protein: 0g

Garden Salsa

9

STOCKS, SAUCES &
STAPLES

PREP TIME:
5 minutes

COOKING
SETTING:
Manual, High
Pressure for
15 minutes
(13 minutes at
sea level)

RELEASE:
Natural for
15 minutes,
then Quick

TOTAL TIME:
35 minutes

DIY VEGETABLE STOCK

BUDGET FRIENDLY • GLUTEN FREE • NUT FREE • SOY FREE

This recipe assumes you're starting from scratch, but if you're the type of home cook who saves veggie trimmings for this very purpose, even better! Add what you have, keeping in mind that different vegetables will change the flavor profile of the finished stock. If you're planning to freeze the stock for later use, consider portioning it into ice cube trays. That way you know each cube is roughly 2 tablespoons of stock, making it easy to use in recipes. **SERVES 8 TO 10**

2 or 3 celery stalks

2 or 3 carrots

1 large onion (I like sweet or yellow; red is a bit too strong)

1 cup mushrooms

6 to 8 whole peppercorns

1 bay leaf

8 cups water

1. In your Instant Pot®, combine the celery, carrots, onion, mushrooms, peppercorns, bay leaf, and water, making sure the veggies are completely covered by water. Lock the lid and turn the steam release handle to Sealing. Using the Manual function, set the cooker to High Pressure for 15 minutes (13 minutes at sea level).

2. When the cook time is complete, let the pressure release naturally for 15 minutes; quick release any remaining pressure.

3. Carefully remove the lid. Strain the stock through a fine-mesh strainer into a large heatproof container. Use immediately or refrigerate in an airtight container for 3 to 4 days, or keep frozen for up to a year.

PER SERVING: Calories: 23; Total fat: 0g; Saturated fat: 0g; Sodium: 23mg; Carbs: 2g; Fiber: 0g; Protein: 0g

BUTTERNUT BASIL RED SAUCE

BUDGET FRIENDLY · NUT FREE · SOY FREE

When I was 21, I moved 3,000 miles away from most of my family. My Uncle Eddie was nearby, and he made these decadent Italian meals every Sunday. His red sauce (or "gravy") turned out to be the cure for homesickness, for which I'll always be grateful! This is my current favorite sauce, a perfect combination of butternut squash, basil, and tomatoes. **MAKES 4 TO 4½ CUPS**

PREP TIME:
10 minutes

COOKING SETTING:
Manual, High Pressure for 20 minutes (17 minutes at sea level)

RELEASE:
Natural for 10 to 15 minutes, then Quick

TOTAL TIME:
45 minutes

1 small butternut squash, peeled and cubed (2 to 3 cups)

2 medium or 3 small tomatoes, quartered

2 garlic cloves, peeled

¼ to ½ cup water (not necessary if your tomatoes are juicy)

4 ounces tomato paste

1 bay leaf

1 teaspoon salt

½ teaspoon freshly ground black pepper

¼ teaspoon baking soda (this helps cut acidity without adding sugar)

Pinch red pepper flakes

½ cup fresh sweet basil leaves, torn

1 to 2 tablespoons fresh Italian parsley leaves

1. In your Instant Pot®, combine the squash, tomatoes, garlic, and water (if using). Top with the tomato paste, bay leaf, salt, pepper, baking soda, and red pepper flakes. There is no need to stir.

2. Lock the lid and turn the steam release handle to Sealing. Using the Manual function, set the cooker to High Pressure for 20 minutes (17 minutes at sea level).

3. When the cook time is complete, let the pressure release naturally for 10 to 15 minutes; quick release any remaining pressure.

4. Carefully remove the lid—your kitchen should smell AMAZING! Let the sauce cool for a few minutes (use mitts or tongs to remove the inner pot). Discard the bay leaf, and add the basil and parsley. Using an immersion blender, blend the sauce until smooth. There may still be a few small intact pieces of basil—I like it that way.

PER SERVING (1 CUP): Calories: 86; Total fat: 0g; Saturated fat: 0g; Sodium: 687mg; Carbs: 21g; Fiber: 4g; Protein: 3g

PREP TIME:
5 minutes

COOKING
SETTING:
Manual, High
Pressure for
20 minutes
(17 minutes at
sea level)

RELEASE:
Natural for
15 minutes,
then Quick

TOTAL TIME:
40 minutes

ALLLL THE GARLIC RED SAUCE

BUDGET FRIENDLY • NUT FREE • SOY FREE

Sure, grocery store sauce is convenient, but with the Instant Pot® in your kitchen so is making your own from scratch. Plus, when you make it, you get to put *allll* the garlic in it. Truly. When it comes to garlic and me, it's go big or go home. You also get to keep out the weird additives found in some mainstream brands. The added bonus is how tantalizing the aroma is after you take off that lid! **MAKES 2½ TO 2¾ CUPS**

---

4 medium (about 1 pound) tomatoes, quartered

1 small sweet onion, peeled and quartered

⅓ cup strong hearty wine (like a Cabernet Sauvignon or Merlot), plus more as needed

½ cup water, plus more as needed

4 ounces tomato paste

4 or 5 garlic cloves, or to taste, peeled

1½ teaspoons dried oregano

1 teaspoon dried basil

1 teaspoon salt

¼ teaspoon baking soda (this helps cut acidity without adding sugar)

Pinch red pepper flakes

---

1. Drop the tomatoes and onion into the Instant Pot®. Add the wine, water, and tomato paste. Cover the veggies with the garlic, oregano, basil, salt, baking soda, and red pepper flakes. There is no need to stir; it's better to have everything mostly on top of the tomatoes than at the bottom of the pot. Lock the lid and turn the steam release handle to Sealing. Using the Manual function, set the cooker to High Pressure for 20 minutes (17 minutes at sea level).

2. When the cook time is complete, turn off the Instant Pot® and let the pressure release naturally for 15 minutes; quick release any remaining pressure.

3. Carefully remove the lid. Using an immersion blender, create the red sauce of your dreams. Add a bit more water (or wine!) if you need to thin it.

PER SERVING (1 CUP): Calories: 149; Total fat: 1g; Saturated fat: 0g; Sodium: 1393mg; Carbs: 27g; Fiber: 7g; Protein: 6g

RED HOT ENCHILADA SAUCE

BUDGET FRIENDLY · GLUTEN FREE · NUT FREE · SOY FREE

Hoo boy, this stuff is spicy! With the poblano and chipotle peppers, the adobo sauce, and the smoked paprika, there is so much hot smoky flavor to adore. Serve this with any favorite Mexican dishes, and I recommend starting your day off right by using this in your next batch of Breakfast Enchiladas (page 34)! **MAKES 3 TO 4 CUPS**

PREP TIME:
10 minutes

COOKING SETTING:
Manual, High Pressure for 10 minutes (9 minutes at sea level)

RELEASE:
Natural

TOTAL TIME:
20 minutes

6 garlic cloves, peeled

2 poblano peppers, chopped

2 tomatoes, chopped

1 or 2 canned chipotle peppers in adobo sauce

½ red onion, chopped

½ cup DIY Vegetable Stock (page 154), or store-bought stock

1 tablespoon adobo sauce from the can

1 teaspoon chili powder (I use a nice New Mexico blend), plus more as needed

1 teaspoon ground cumin

1 teaspoon salt

1 teaspoon apple cider vinegar

½ teaspoon smoked paprika

8 ounces tomato paste

1. In your Instant Pot®, combine the garlic, poblanos, tomatoes, chipotles, red onion, stock, adobo sauce, chili powder, cumin, salt, vinegar, and paprika. Stir well. Spoon the tomato paste on top, without mixing it in. Lock the lid and turn the steam release handle to Sealing. Using the Manual function, set the cooker to High Pressure for 10 minutes (9 minutes at sea level).

2. When the cook time is complete, turn off the Instant Pot® and let the pressure release naturally until the pin drops.

3. Carefully remove the lid. Using an immersion blender. There may still be a few small intact pieces of basil—I like it that way.

INGREDIENT TIP: If you want less heat, skip the chili powder and substitute green bell pepper for one or both of the poblanos.

PER SERVING (½ CUP): Calories: 62; Total fat: 1g; Saturated fat: 0g; Sodium: 544mg; Carbs: 13g; Fiber: 3g; Protein: 3g

PREP TIME:
10 minutes

COOKING
SETTING:
Manual, High
Pressure for
5 minutes
(4 minutes
at sea level);
Sauté Low for
5 minutes

RELEASE:
Quick

TOTAL TIME:
20 minutes

POBLANO CHEEZE SAUCE

BUDGET FRIENDLY • SOY FREE

Ohhhh, this sauce. Hyperbole aside, this is the best vegan cheese sauce I've ever tasted . . . and I've eaten a LOT of vegan cheese, It's rich and not too spicy, but the roasted poblanos add a delicious smoky flavor. **MAKES 3 CUPS**

1 medium sweet potato,
peeled and chopped

1 cup water

1 cup raw cashews,
soaked in water overnight,
drained, and rinsed well

1 cup unsweetened nondairy
milk (I like cashew)

¼ cup nutritional yeast

1 tablespoon apple cider vinegar

2 teaspoons salt

¼ teaspoon garlic powder

Pinch freshly
ground black pepper

2 poblano peppers, roasted

Chili powder, to taste (optional)

1. In your Instant Pot®, combine the sweet potato and water. Lock the lid and turn the steam release handle to Sealing. Using the Manual function, set the cooker to High Pressure for 5 minutes (4 minutes at sea level).

2. When the cook time is complete, quick release the pressure.

3. Carefully remove the lid and drain the water from the pot.

4. In a high-speed blender or food processor, combine the cashews, milk, nutritional yeast, vinegar, salt, garlic powder, and pepper. Blend until completely smooth. Add the sweet potatoes and blend again. Finally, add the poblanos and pulse just until there are green specks throughout.

5. Pour the blended mixture back into the Instant Pot®. Using a rubber spatula, make sure you get as much as possible. Select Sauté Low. When the sauce is hot, turn off the Instant Pot®. Taste and adjust the seasonings. If you want more heat, add chili powder to taste.

PER SERVING (½ CUP): Calories: 200; Total fat: 12g; Saturated fat: 2g; Sodium: 825mg; Carbs: 16g; Fiber: 4g; Protein: 8g

GARDEN SALSA

BUDGET FRIENDLY · GLUTEN FREE · NUT FREE · SOY FREE

I find the salsa aisle in my local grocery store a bit overwhelming. So many brands and flavors to choose from, and how do I know it won't be too spicy for my sometimes-wimpy palate? This is why, for barbecues and Mexican-themed dinners, I always make my own. It guarantees your salsa will be delicious and fresh, and I actually find it relaxing to chop all those veggies. This version is fairly mild, so feel free to add hotter chile peppers or chili powder. **MAKES 6 TO 8 CUPS**

PREP TIME:
5 minutes

COOKING SETTING:
Manual, High Pressure for 5 minutes (4 minutes at sea level)

RELEASE:
Natural for 10 minutes, then Quick

TOTAL TIME:
20 minutes

8 large tomatoes (I use multiple kinds of tomatoes in this, so if you're using any smaller tomatoes, just make sure the total amount is roughly the equivalent of 8 large tomatoes), roughly chopped

5 or 6 garlic cloves, finely diced

2 jalapeño peppers, seeded and diced

1 bell pepper, any color, diced

1 small red onion, diced

1 small yellow onion, diced

1 tablespoon ground cumin

3 to 4 teaspoons salt

Generous ½ teaspoon freshly ground black pepper

½ teaspoon baking soda

¼ cup tomato paste

2 tablespoons freshly squeezed lime juice

Chopped fresh cilantro leaves, to taste

1. In your Instant Pot®, stir together the tomatoes, garlic, jalapeños, bell pepper, red onion, yellow onion, cumin, salt, pepper, and baking soda. Lock the lid and turn the steam release handle to Sealing. Using the Manual function, set the cooker to High Pressure for 5 minutes (4 minutes at sea level).

2. When the cook time is complete, let the pressure release naturally for 10 minutes; quick release any remaining pressure.

3. Carefully remove the lid and stir in the tomato paste, lime juice, and cilantro. Let cool completely before serving.

PREPARATION TIP: Use your food processor to speed up all the veggie chopping!

PER SERVING (½ CUP): Calories: 43; Total fat: 0g; Saturated fat: 0g; Sodium: 541mg; Carbs: 9g; Fiber: 2g; Protein: 2g

CASHEW SOUR CREAM

BUDGET FRIENDLY · GLUTEN FREE

I eat this sour cream a lot. A LOT. Obviously it's terrific atop pretty much any Mexican food, but it's also perfect for stirring into pastas where you want a bit of creaminess, like my Kimchi Pasta (page 138) or Mushroom Kale Stroganoff (page 126). A lot of recipes in this book either call for sour cream or suggest it as an additional topping, so if you don't already have cashews in your fridge, I suggest a quick trip to the store. **SERVES 4 TO 6**

1 cup raw cashews, soaked in water overnight, drained, and rinsed well

Juice of 1 lemon, plus more as needed

¼ cup nondairy milk, plus more as needed

1½ teaspoons apple cider vinegar

½ teaspoon salt, plus more as needed

In a blender, combine the cashews, lemon juice, milk, vinegar, and salt. Blend until completely smooth. Taste and add more salt or lemon juice as desired. If you want a thinner cream, add a little more milk. Keep refrigerated in an airtight container for 4 to 6 days.

INGREDIENT TIP: Raw cashews should be kept refrigerated in an airtight container (I use a resealable plastic bag), and will last for up to 6 months. They'll even last for a year if frozen!

PER SERVING: Calories: 222; Total fat: 17g; Saturated fat: 3g; Sodium: 308mg; Carbs: 11g; Fiber: 1g; Protein: 7g

MUSHROOM GRAVY

BUDGET FRIENDLY · GLUTEN FREE · NUT FREE · SOY FREE

I didn't really learn to cook until my thirties. This is fairly embarrassing to admit (especially in my own cookbook), but I want to illustrate how very easy this from-scratch gravy is to make. I had always leaned heavily on premade gravy because making my own seemed daunting. But it couldn't be simpler. A few minutes of sautéing, then the Instant Pot® does the work while you focus on the rest of the meal! **SERVES 4 TO 6**

PREP TIME:
5 minutes

COOKING SETTING:
Sauté Low for 5 minutes; Manual, High Pressure for 20 minutes (17 minutes at sea level)

RELEASE:
Natural for 10 minutes, then Quick

TOTAL TIME:
40 minutes

1 tablespoon olive oil

8 ounces baby bella mushrooms, diced

½ small sweet onion, diced

2 garlic cloves, minced

2 tablespoons vegan Worcestershire sauce

1 teaspoon Dijon mustard

1 teaspoon rubbed sage

1 teaspoon Montreal chicken seasoning

1¼ cups DIY Vegetable Stock (page 154), or store-bought stock, divided

¼ cup red wine

1 tablespoon cornstarch

1. On your Instant Pot®, select Sauté Low. When the display reads "Hot," add the oil and heat until it shimmers. Add the mushrooms and onion. Sauté for 2 to 3 minutes, stirring frequently. Turn off the Instant Pot® and add the garlic. Cook, stirring so it doesn't burn, for 30 seconds more.

2. Add the Worcestershire sauce, mustard, sage, Montreal chicken seasoning, ¾ cup of stock, and the red wine. Lock the lid and turn the steam release handle to Sealing. Using the Manual function, set the cooker to High Pressure for 20 minutes (17 minutes at sea level).

3. When the cook time is complete, let the pressure release naturally for 10 minutes; quick release any remaining pressure.

4. In a small bowl, whisk the remaining ½ cup of stock and cornstarch. Carefully remove the lid and stir this slurry into the gravy. Select Sauté Low again and simmer the gravy for 2 to 3 minutes until thickened.

PER SERVING: Calories: 76; Total fat: 4g; Saturated fat: 1g; Sodium: 366mg; Carbs: 7g; Fiber: 1g; Protein: 2g

ALTITUDE ADJUSTMENTS FOR THE PRESSURE COOKER

Adjusting cooking times based on your altitude is not an exact science, but the accepted guideline is that "cooking time under pressure should be increased by 5 percent for every 1,000 feet after 2,000 feet above sea level." (Anderson, B. M. [1980] *The New High Altitude Cookbook).*

What does this mean for you? The recipes in this book were developed in Colorado at an altitude of just over 5,000 feet above sea level. I've also provided the cook times for those of you at 0 to 2,000 feet above sea level, which are decreased by 15 percent. Use the following chart and my original cook times to decrease or increase the cook times accordingly.

The good news is, the Instant Pot® is very forgiving when it comes to cook times, especially if you aim low. If you open the lid and the ingredients are slightly undercooked, you can always bring the Instant Pot® back to pressure. You can also add more liquid as needed and use the Sauté function to continue the cooking process.

ALTITUDE ABOVE SEA LEVEL	ADJUST COOK TIME BY
0 to 2,000 feet	Decrease by 15 percent
3,000 feet	Decrease by 10 percent
4,000 feet	Decrease by 5 percent
5,000 feet	No Change
6,000 feet	Increase by 5 percent
7,000 feet	Increase by 10 percent
8,000 feet	Increase by 15 percent
9,000 feet	Increase by 20 percent
10,000 feet	Increase by 25 percent

THE DIRTY DOZEN AND THE CLEAN FIFTEEN™

A nonprofit environmental watchdog organization called Environmental Working Group (EWG) looks at data supplied by the US Department of Agriculture (USDA) and the Food and Drug Administration (FDA) about pesticide residues. Each year it compiles a list of the best and worst pesticide loads found in commercial crops. You can use these lists to decide which fruits and vegetables to buy organic to minimize your exposure to pesticides and which produce is considered safe enough to buy conventionally. This does not mean they are pesticide-free, though, so wash these fruits and vegetables thoroughly. The list is updated annually, and you can find it online at EWG.org/FoodNews.

DIRTY DOZEN

1. strawberries
2. spinach
3. kale
4. nectarines
5. apples
6. grapes
7. peaches
8. cherries
9. pears
10. tomatoes
11. celery
12. potatoes

†Additionally, nearly three-quarters of hot pepper samples contained pesticide residues.

CLEAN FIFTEEN™

1. avocados
2. sweet corn*
3. pineapples
4. sweet peas (frozen)
5. onions
6. papayas*
7. eggplants
8. asparagus
9. kiwis
10. cabbages
11. cauliflower
12. cantaloupes
13. broccoli
14. mushrooms
15. honeydew melons

* A small amount of sweet corn, papaya, and summer squash sold in the United States is produced from genetically modified seeds. Buy organic varieties of these crops if you want to avoid genetically modified produce.

MEASUREMENT CONVERSIONS

VOLUME EQUIVALENTS (LIQUID)

US STANDARD	US STANDARD (OUNCES)	METRIC (APPROXIMATE)
2 tablespoons	1 fl. oz.	30 mL
¼ cup	2 fl. oz.	60 mL
½ cup	4 fl. oz.	120 mL
1 cup	8 fl. oz.	240 mL
1½ cups	12 fl. oz.	355 mL
2 cups or 1 pint	16 fl. oz.	475 mL
4 cups or 1 quart	32 fl. oz.	1 L

OVEN TEMPERATURES

FAHRENHEIT (F)	CELSIUS (C) (APPROXIMATE)
250°F	120°C
300°F	150°C
325°F	165°C
350°F	180°C
375°F	190°C
400°F	200°C
425°F	220°C

VOLUME EQUIVALENTS (DRY)

US STANDARD	METRIC (APPROXIMATE)
⅛ teaspoon	0.5 mL
¼ teaspoon	1 mL
½ teaspoon	2 mL
¾ teaspoon	4 mL
1 teaspoon	5 mL
1 tablespoon	15 mL
¼ cup	59 mL
⅓ cup	79 mL
½ cup	118 mL
⅔ cup	156 mL
¾ cup	177 mL
1 cup	235 mL
2 cups or 1 pint	475 mL
3 cups	700 mL
4 cups or 1 quart	1 L
½ gallon	2 L
1 gallon	4 L

WEIGHT EQUIVALENTS

US STANDARD	METRIC (APPROXIMATE)
½ ounce	15 grams
1 ounce	30 grams
2 ounces	60 grams
4 ounces	115 grams
8 ounces	225 grams
12 ounces	340 grams
16 ounces or 1 pound	455 grams

RESOURCES

We live in the age of information, and there are so many great resources out there for home cooks and their Instant Pots®! Here are a few I turn to again and again:

- InstantPot.com (of course!)
- JLGoesVegan.com
- TheVeggieQueen.com

- PressureCookRecipes.com
- HipPressureCooking.com
- Reddit.com/r/PressureCooking

REFERENCES

ANDERSON, BEVERLEY M. *The New High Altitude Cookbook.* New York: Random House, 1980.

CHOI. Y., S. M. LEE, J CHUN, H. B. LEE, AND J. LEE. "Influence of Heat Treatment on the Anti-oxidant Activities and Polyphenolic Compounds of Shiitake (*Lentinus edodes)* Mushroom." *Food Chemistry* 99, no. 2 (2006): 381–387. doi:10.1016/j.foodchem.2005.08.004.

HIPPRESSURECOOKING.COM

INDEX

ACKNOWLEDGMENTS

I'VE SPENT A LOT OF MY LIFE writing, mostly short stories, and always dreamed of becoming a published author. Well, here I am! Making this book a reality was harder than I imagined and more fulfilling than I dreamed, and I have so much gratitude for everyone who helped make it possible.

Thank you to my friends and my crazy family for always putting up with me. Jason Musick, who has supported my vegan journey from day one—without you, there would've been no blog, and thus no book! Dad and Grandma Josie, I miss you both every day and I know you're looking down and cheering for me always. Bobby and Tony, I'm glad you moved to Colorado so I can cook for you—I appreciate that omnivore support! And especially, thank you to my mom, who is my favorite person on the planet and to whom I owe absolutely everything.

A round of applause for my friends who stepped up to be sous chefs, recipe testers, and tasters: Jamie Hostetter, Denise Lindom, and Cynthia Thayer—your help, support, and feedback are so very much appreciated.

And to my editor, Bridget Fitzgerald, who has been so kind and supportive as I learned my way through this, and the entire Callisto Media team: Thank you!

ABOUT THE AUTHOR

BARB MUSICK lives in Colorado with her pack of rescue pets. She shares her adventures and love of food, travel, and animals on her blog, *That Was Vegan?*, along with vegan recipes everyone will love. Visit her at ThatWasVegan.com.